LEADING IN THE NHS

A Practical Guide

LEADING IN THE NHS

A Practical Guide

Second Edition

Rosemary Stewart

MACMILLAN
Business

First edition 1989
Reprinted 1993
Second edition 1996

Published by
MACMILLAN PRESS LTD
Houndmills, Basingstoke, Hampshire RG21 6XS
and London
Companies and representatives
throughout the world

ISBN 0–333–65575–3 hardcover
ISBN 0–333–65576–1 paperback

A catalogue record for this book is available
from the British Library.

10   9   8   7   6   5   4   3
05   04   03   02   01   00   99   98   97

Printed in Great Britain by
Antony Rowe Ltd.,
Chippenham, Wiltshire.

Contents

In Conclusion   200

List of figures

Guide to reading this book

This guide seeks to save your time by telling you how to find what will most interest you. This will depend upon your preferences and your job.

Those who prefer practice should start with the case studies. Those who find theory more helpful or who like a mix of theory and practice should read the book in the order that it is written.

Readers from different backgrounds, and at different stages in their career, can use this book, but they should use it differently, hence this guide.

1. *If you want to skim the book* – Read the Introduction, Contents page, Summary and **bold type** passages of Chapter 1, the Summaries of the chapters that interest you, and the comments 'In Conclusion'.
2. *If you only want to read what is most relevant to you* – Everyone read the Introduction, Contents page, comments 'In Conclusion' (p. 200) and at least the Summary of Chapter 1.

Who you are	What to read
Junior and middle managers in any profession	Chapters 1, 2, 6, 10, 11, 12, 13, 14 and **bold type** passages and Summaries of Chapters 3, 4, 9
Senior nurses	Chapters 1, 2, 3, 6, 13, 14 and **bold type** passages and Summaries of Chapters 4, 9 If you like Case Studies, read Chapters 11 and 12 especially cases 5 and 6
Doctors	Chapters 1, 2, 4, 6 and **bold type** passages and Summary of Chapter 3 Chapters 13 and 14 and cases 7–11 for those involved in management

Chief executives and other senior managers	Chapter 1 Start with the Summary of each chapter, and then read the chapters and the case studies that interest you
Chair	Chapters 1, 3, 4, 5, 6, 7 and Summary of Chapters 8, 9 You may find the Case Studies of chief executives of interest, nos 1, 2 and Chapter 12
Non-executive directors	Chapters 3, 4, 7, 9
Those involved in management development in and for the NHS	Chapters 1, 10–14 and the chapters on relationships that are relevant to those with whom you are working
Students	Chapters 1, 2, 6, 10, 11, 12, 14 and any of the others relevant to your course
Others working with the NHS	Chapter 9 You may also find Chapter 12 of interest
Others	Chapters 1, 2, 6, 13, 14 are of value to managers in other organizations and to management students

List of abbreviations

BMA	British Medical Association
BMJ	British Medical Journal
CHC	Community Health Council
DA	District Administrator
DGM	District General Manager
GP	General Practitioner
GPF	General Practitioner Fundholding
JCC	Joint Consultative Committee
ICI	Imperial Chemical Industry
MP	Member of Parliament
NAHA	National Association of Health Authorities
NHS	National Health Service
NHSE	National Health Service Executive
NHSME	National Health Service Management Executive
OPCS	Office of Population Censuses and Surveys
RHA	Regional Health Authority

Acknowledgements

My earlier debts were acknowledged in the first edition. Most important, of course, were my fellow researchers on the study of district general managers whose names are given in Appendix A.

My thanks for the second edition go primarily to those interviewed for the case studies in Chapters 10 and 11 which replace the earlier case studies. I enjoyed meeting them, where that was possible, and hearing what they had to say about leadership.

I am also grateful to Heather-Jane Sears for commenting on Chapter 3, Leadership and Nurses, and to Adrian Pollitt for commenting on Chapter 8 on Leading in the Regional Office. Of course the responsibility for the views expressed, and for the remaining defects are mine.

Maggie Latham, Secretary of the Oxford Health Care Management Institute, Templeton College has done the dreary work of preparing the book for the publisher with efficiency and good humour. I am most grateful to her for both these qualities.

ROSEMARY STEWART

Introduction to the first edition

This book has a mission. This mission is to persuade you, the reader, that the NHS needs leadership and that you should be leading, and preparing yourself to be a better leader. There *are* opportunities for leadership even in junior jobs. My mission is also to help you to understand leadership, to think boldly about what you could achieve and to suggest ways of doing so. It is a guide to leading the different groups that make up the NHS.

My aim is to encourage you to think highly of your role, to lift your head above the immediate pressures and to see yourself as a *leader*. My message is for present and potential leaders at all levels in the NHS and in all occupations. It is also for Authority members, as you can encourage your managers to be leaders, as well as at times making a leadership contribution yourself.

This book is written because I believe – passionately – that leadership at all levels in the NHS is required to overcome the defeatist tendencies that have been a characteristic of the NHS over the years.[1]

In 1984–5 the introduction of general management into the NHS led to a major reorganization. The 1989 NHS review means more radical change. Leadership is now both more necessary, and more possible, than in the past. Management and administration remain necessary and it is important that they are well done. What is new is the growing need for leadership to help staff, whatever their professional background, to tackle the new situations with which they are faced.

Most books for NHS readers are about functions like planning, about resource allocation or structures. Surprisingly few are about the *people* in the NHS.[2] Yet the work of organizations gets done mainly through people, particularly in a service like the NHS. Changes affect people and to be implemented successfully require their support. Enthusiastic commitment and well directed energy are the marks of well led organizations that cope successfully with changes whatever their cause. Leadership can generate this commitment: leaders to do this are needed at all levels in the NHS.

The book originates from a two and a half year study, from 1985–7, of a sample of 20 District General Managers (DGMs) in the NHS in England

and Wales,[3] from an earlier study of District Administrators (DAs),[4] from a current study of changes affecting middle managers in all kinds of organizations, and from the author's experience of teaching managers in industry, commerce and the public service (including the NHS), how to review their effectiveness. The author has also co-directed an international conference on leadership.[5]

Part 1, Chapter 1 describes the *concept* of leadership, and how it differs from management and administration, though all three are needed in the NHS. Part II is about *how to lead* the different kinds of individuals and groups with whom leaders in the NHS may have to work. Its introduction describes five common reasons for friction, and gives some general guidance on managing relationships and managing change. Each of the chapters in Part II has a common format:

1. A statement of the *ideal to aim at*.
2. *Difficulties* likely to be encountered in achieving the ideal.
3. Steps to be taken towards achieving the ideal.

These steps are based on the experience of leaders in the NHS and in other organizations. You can use the statement of the ideal as a checklist of points when deciding on *your own*. You can use the account of the difficulties as a warning of those problems you may need to *overcome*. The statement of steps to be taken will help you to decide how to *achieve* your ideal.

Part III gives *practical examples* of leadership in the NHS. Chapter 9 is based on interviews with young leaders in different occupations within the NHS and at different levels. There are questions at the end so that you can consider their relevance for you. Chapter 10 is a more detailed Case Study of a DGM which describes both his own views on, and his practice of, leadership and how his main contacts described and assessed his approach. The accounts of young leaders are there to encourage young readers to follow their example, and older managers to remember the importance of identifying and developing potential leaders. The Case Studies are there as examples of how different leaders tackle their jobs.

Part IV is intended to help you to become a *more effective leader*. Chapter 11 is about managing yourself and your job, and provides a variety of suggestions and models for doing so. It is therefore about management as well as leadership. It emphasises the need to *improve your understanding* – of yourself, of your job and of ways of becoming more effective in your job. Chapter 12 is about how to develop yourself. The final comments, In Conclusion, are intended to encourage you to *act* on what you have read.

Knowing how busy you are, the book is designed to be read in two ways: to be *skimmed* for its main messages or to be *read* for its detailed help in deciding what you want to achieve, what difficulties you will have to overcome, and how to go about it. The Guide to Reading this book on pp. viii–ix will help you to identify the sections that are most relevant to you, depending on your position.

References are mainly given to acknowledge a quotation, or when the reader may be looking for help. The book is addressed to you, not to fellow academics, though they may find some sections useful for teaching in managerial programmes.

The book follows others in avoiding exclusive use of 'he' for men and women by the use of both 'she' and 'he', by the use of the plural, and sometimes of 'he' and 'she'. I have used the term 'Chairman' because that is still the official description for men and women who are appointed to chair their Authorities.

Templeton College, Oxford   ROSEMARY STEWART
February 1989

Notes

1.   Enoch Powell, for three years a Minister of Health, wrote in the early 1960s, that the NHS 'presents what must be the unique spectacle of an undertaking that is run down by everyone engaged in it.' That would be an extreme statement now, and no doubt was then, but unfortunately this distinctive characteristic of the NHS remains. Quotation from Joe Rogaly 'Hearts, Minds and Wallets', in the *Financial Times*, 22 January 1988, for Enoch Powell's book *Medicine and Politics* (London: Pitman Medical, 1975).
2.   One of the exceptions is Robert J. Maxwell and Victor Morrison (eds), 'Working with People' (King Edward's Hospital Fund for London, 1983).
3.   This study was funded by the NHSTA, and published by them in 1987 and 1988 as the Templeton Series on DGMs in nine Issue Studies (see Appendix A).
4.   Rosemary Stewart, Peter Smith, Jenny Blake and Pauline Wingate, 'The District Administrator in the National Health Service' (King Edward's Hospital Fund for London, 1980).
5.   Papers published in James G. Hunt, Dian-Marie Hosking, Chester A. Schriesheim and Rosemary Stewart, *Leaders and Managers: International Perspectives on Managerial Behaviours and Leadership* (New York: Pergamon Press, 1984).

Introduction to the second edition

Much has changed in the NHS since the late 1980s, hence the need for a new edition. The aim of the book remains the same but much of the content has had to be changed.

New case studies are needed to take account of the many new jobs and new opportunities for leadership in the new NHS. For one case study it was appropriate to do a part two to illustrate new opportunities for senior nurses. This time four of the case studies are of doctors, to reflect the much greater role that doctors are now playing in management and the new leadership opportunities for GPs. It is noteworthy that it was much easier this time to find people of 35 or less who qualified as young leaders in senior positions – doctors being a partial exception because of their long training.

Changes in the ways of working are reflected in the addition of a new chapter on Leadership in Teams and by the changes in title and emphasis to the chapter previously called 'Leading Subordinates' and now called 'Leading Staff'. Substantial changes were needed for the chapters on nurses, doctors, the DHA (now the board), and the region. Each of these chapters now has an introduction which discusses the implications of recent changes. More minor changes were made to the other chapters. Since chair has now become more common it is used in place of chairman, except in the case studies where the latter was the word used by the individual interviewed.

What has remained the same is the discussion on leadership in Chapter 1 and the framework for the first ten chapters of: the ideals to aim at, the difficulties in the way of achieving them and steps towards them. The book is still divided into four parts, as described in the original introduction. A guide for busy readers on how to find what will interest them is retained, so are chapter summaries and the highlighting of key points. There are questions to be used with the examples in Part

III to help students and others interested in considering the lessons that they can draw from others' experience.

Oxford Health Care Management Institute,   ROSEMARY STEWART
Templeton College, Oxford
April 1995

PART I

THE CONCEPT OF LEADERSHIP

CHAPTER 1

Leadership

'*There is a difference between leadership and management. Leadership is of the spirit, compounded of personality and vision; its practice is an art. Management is of the mind, a matter of accurate calculation...its practice is a science. Managers are necessary; leaders are essential.*'
(Field Marshall Lord Slim, when Governor-General of Australia)[1]

Leadership, management and administration

In difficult times, people need leadership as well as management. This is true in the NHS today, and in the foreseeable future. It is true, too, in many other organizations in Britain and elsewhere. Yet 'leadership' is a word that many in the NHS are still chary of using. Even 'management' may still be viewed with scepticism and the traditional term, 'administration' used instead, especially by doctors referring to non-medical managers. Each word has a different, though often ambiguous, meaning and each is necessary in the NHS today. Before we can focus on leadership, we must first understand how these terms differ.

LEADERSHIP

The word 'leadership' has an emotive character that 'management' and 'administration' lack, and usually the emotions are positive ones. Most of us think that we can recognize leadership, though we may not find it easy to define.

Leadership is *discovering the route ahead* and encouraging and – personality permitting – inspiring others to follow. Hence leadership is most needed in changing times, when the way ahead is not clear. A good leader should both show the way and make others feel enthusiastic about following it. Change can then, depending on its nature, become positive, exciting and challenging rather than discouraging and threatening. Leadership should be fun, some of the time, both for the leader and for the followers.

Managers have staff. Leaders have followers: people who recognize and find attractive the leader's sense of purpose. Leaders are those who can get the people with whom they work to be convinced cooperators. Leaders make others feel that what they are doing matters and hence makes them feel good about their work. Taking this description as a guide, look around you at work and ask yourself: 'who are the leaders?' Who are enthusiastic about what they do and convey that enthusiasm to others? You will notice at once that some of the leaders are not those of the highest status. **You can give a lead from any position, though the more authority you have the more important it is that you should be a good leader.**

MANAGEMENT

Good management is also important for the NHS. This was a major reason for the introduction of general managers in the later 1980s. Good management makes it possible for the leader's vision to be implemented by providing the discipline of objectives, targets and reviews to make the vision *concrete*. Management is different from leadership, though leadership is an aspect of management, an aspect that is essential in changing situations and less important in stable periods.

Management is a set of techniques and approaches that can be learnt. It involves planning, which includes strategy and setting objectives. There are textbooks that tell you how to plan and about the related process of budgeting. Organizing, in the sense of creating formal structures and procedures, is also part of management. Textbooks can help the manager to decide what form of organization is appropriate for the tasks to be done and the environment in which they have to be carried out. Motivating and controlling are two other classic management functions, along with co-ordination. Management textbooks and management consultants can advise on motivational strategies, on the techniques for controlling and on the methods of coordination. Plenty of such textbooks exist, including two by the author,[2] so this book does not describe such managerial functions.

The NHS has been deficient in the knowledge and practice of management, though these are essential for the effective use of resources. Gradually senior staff have come to be called managers rather than officers. They have learnt to think more like managers: to recognize the importance of deciding what has to be done and of ensuring that it gets done by agreeing objectives, establishing priorities and target dates, and monitoring whether plans are being implemented. Gradually, too, managers in the NHS are learning to be more concerned with cost effectiveness. More slowly, they are recognizing the influence that they have on staff motivation and their responsibility for creating an environment where staff feel well motivated. This is where leadership rather than purely managerial ability can help.

ADMINISTRATION

In the past, only administration was thought to be necessary in public service; hence the public service had administrators and companies had managers and sometimes leaders too. **Administration is the carrying out of policies, and being publicly accountable for doing so**. Public accountability means that administration involves more paperwork than management, because there needs to be written evidence of what is done, and why.

Public accountability remains, so administration is still needed. Managers should ensure that there is efficient administration. It will often be done more efficiently by one of their staff, provided they choose the right person, than by themselves. **Good managers are not necessarily good administrators, and a leader has a more important role to play away from the desk**.

1. Administrators **confirm in writing**.
2. Managers **direct**.
3. Leaders **point the way**: they identify and symbolize what is important.

These descriptions exemplify the different approaches involved, though leaders will also have to manage. There are situations – though rare in the NHS today – where leadership is not required. **Whether you need to lead as well as to manage depends upon which of the following is your most important responsibility**:

1. maintaining stability, so managing *variations*;
2. managing *improvement*;
3. *radical change*.

Administrators should be able to cope with the first, managers with the second. It is *leaders* who are needed for more radical change and for coping with a difficult environment. The radical changes affecting the NHS make good leaders at all levels essential.

Characteristics of leadership

POINTING THE WAY

This is the leader's *first task*. Leaders can only point the way if they know the direction that they want to go. When you start in a new job, it may be all too clear what needs to be done. Sometimes that will not be so. This can be true for those charged with introducing changes that they do not fully understand. It can be true, too, for those who have been in the job a long time and do not see any new paths ahead. Subsequent chapters suggest the ideals to aim at which you can use as a starting point.

It helps to have a picture – what in writings on leadership is called a 'vision' – of where we want our part of the organization to be in the future. (It is not only writers who use that word – Shell, for example, has been using 'visioning' as a process for some years.) Warren Bennis and Burt Nanus in their book on leadership explain what a vision is as follows:

> a vision articulates a view of a realistic, credible, attractive future for the organization, a condition that is better in some important ways than what now exists...With a vision, the leader provides the all-important bridge from the present to the future of the organization.[3]

They see having a vision of what you want to achieve as distinguishing a leader from a manager:

> By focusing attention on a vision, the leader operates on the *emotional and spiritual resources* of the organization, on its values, commitment, and aspirations. The manager, by contrast, operates on the *physical resources* of the organization... An excellent manager can see to it that work is done productively and efficiently, on schedule, and with a high level of quality. It remains for the effective leader, however, to help people in the organization know pride and satisfaction in their work.[4]

SYMBOLIZING WHAT MATTERS

An essential role for a leader is to symbolize the *meaning* and *values* of an organization – one chief executive described himself as the 'keeper of the flame'. It is for this reason that a visible leader is important in encouraging others to contribute wholeheartedly to the goals of the organization. **Leaders show clearly what they care about.**

GETTING OTHERS TO SHARE YOUR IDEALS

Leadership means getting people to share the ideals, to attach the same meanings to what is happening and what needs to be done. As Gareth Morgan, a Canadian professor of administrative studies, puts it:

> the process of becoming a leader ultimately hinges on the ability to create a shared sense of reality.[5]

And also, as Warren Bennis, an American professor, who has written about leadership over many years, says:

> The leader must be a social architect who studies and shapes what is called 'the culture of work' – those intangibles that are so hard to discern but so terribly important in governing the way people act, the values and norms that are subtly transmitted to individuals and groups and that tend to create binding and bonding.[6]

CREATING PRIDE IN THE ORGANIZATION

Leadership involves getting people to identify with their part of the organization and to feel proud of where they work. This is an aspect of leadership that the armed services understand well.

Pride is linked to achievement and high standards. It is about being able to say – and being enthusiastic about saying – how we excel. Leadership sets high goals and is not content with statements like: 'we compare favourably with', and still less: 'we are no worse than'.

MAKING PEOPLE FEEL IMPORTANT

This is closely linked to the next characteristic of leadership, of *realizing people's potential*. **People have more energy and will set themselves higher standards if they think that they, and what they do, *matter*.** Feeling good about what you are doing is a major incentive. Achieving this does not require special skill, but an ability to treat each person as a distinct and valued individual.

REALIZING PEOPLE'S POTENTIAL

Leaders in an organization should be providing the environment – the *culture* – within which people's energies are released and they feel able to innovate. This is 'empowering' others to perform, a fashionable word that has its roots in Douglas McGregor's *Theory Y*. Writing in 1960 he said:

> the limits on human collaboration in the organizational setting are not limits of human nature but of management's ingenuity in discovering how to realize the potential represented by its human resources.[7]

This is a lesson that many managers still find it hard to learn despite all the writings, teaching and practical examples that have reinforced it since McGregor wrote.

Leaders do not necessarily have to lead from the front. They can share leadership, as Chapter 6 on Sharing the Leadership: Team Working describes. **One of a leader's responsibilities is to develop leadership qualities in others by giving them opportunities to lead**. This means giving them the space and the opportunities to grow.

SELF-SUFFICIENCY

Being a leader can be lonely. You have to take tough decisions which may be unpopular as well as painful for individuals. So, you must not be too dependent upon being liked. You will also have to take risky decisions. **You must learn to accept yourself and to rely on yourself**. When you fail you may need to accept that you did your best.

Leadership requires some innate abilities, but less than is popularly thought. **Many readers could lead provided they knew what they wanted to achieve and could communicate that to others**. You can learn to recognize when leadership is required. You can also develop your understanding of yourself and of others, so that you know what you can best contribute.

As John Van Maurik has put it:

> Being a leader is something you *do* rather than something you are. It is the ability to bring out a number of talents and to operate effectively through other people, making them gladly accept your goals while still having the freedom to do things their way.[8]

Why leadership is necessary

Much more is now expected of managers in most organizations, including the NHS, than it was in the past. Hence the need for them to be leaders who can show the way and help others to adapt successfully to the changing environment within which they work.

The NHS needs leaders to help people to cope – and to cope without discouragement – with the difficulties that confront it (and, indeed, any method of providing health care). It needs leaders who will do much more than that, however, who will think positively about what they can do to improve the Service, not merely negatively about how they can survive within limited resources.

The changes affecting the NHS have come from a variety of sources. Some stemmed from the policies of Conservative governments; others from the general problems of providing health care in affluent countries, and yet others from the rapid changes in medical technology. The common pressures upon health care whatever the system of provision are well known. They include the larger number of old people, particularly the very old, the rise in chronic sickness, the discovery of new, and often very expensive, ways of treating people and more knowledgeable and demanding patients. It is these problems that led a conference of health service academics, from France, the USA, Quebec and Britain, to publish their proceedings in 1984 under the title *The End of an Illusion:*[9] the illusion being that it was possible to provide everyone with all the health care that they wanted. Over a decade later we are all too aware of the financial limitations to what can be done, hence the discussion about how to ration care.

It is the *extent* and *rapidity* of change affecting many kinds of organizations that makes leadership so important today. This is widely recognized. In the UK, for example, there has been a growth of courses on leadership for managers at all levels. These take many different forms including being tested physically and psychologically in unfamiliar and exhausting conditions. One example of the interest in developing leadership ability at the top is that for many years a one-week programme on top management leadership has been regularly sold out at Templeton College, the Oxford Centre for Management Studies. Another example is the number of new books published in the USA in the late 1980s and early 1990s arguing that American companies urgently need to improve their leadership capacity.

The changes affecting the NHS have parallels in other organizations: without this recognition it is easier to feel hard done by. There have been, and are, major changes affecting managers in industry and commerce that stem from the great increase in competitive pressure, the internationalization of business, the threat of acquisition, the rapidity of product change especially in the newer industries and the growth of information technology. In the public sector the growing cost of a welfare state is a major concern in many countries, despite the reduction in defence expenditure.

There are similar kinds of responses to these pressures so that **leaders in very different kinds of organizations are trying to manage similar kinds of change**. The uncertainties and insecurities are similar too, as change often has to be managed in a context of job insecurity for many, often including the leaders. The rhetoric behind the changes is the same in the public and the private sector, for example: devolution, empowerment, team working and total quality.

A common aim of many of the changes both within companies and in the public service is to increase sensitivity to customer needs. In companies, this is seen as an important way of competing effectively. In the public service, it has been politically inspired, and is a response to the growth of a more knowledgeable and demanding public leading to the end of 'the grateful society' when the recipients of public service were expected to be grateful for any help they received.

There are four main challenges to leaders in the NHS. First, to envision what should be done by them and those who work with them to make their part of the Service better. Second, to realize, as the quotation above from Douglas McGregor says, the potential in human resources. Third, to respond to a more knowledgeable and demanding public. Fourth, to help junior staff to share in the excitement of change rather than to feel demoralized by it.

Finding the way forward

'Where there is no vision, the people perish.'

(*Proverbs* xxix. 18)

The new demands on managers are reflected in the use of different words for talking about what they need to do. One of these is 'vision': a word that many would have thought to be odd, even quite inappropriate, in the 1970s or even the early 1980s. Now its value is as a spur for thinking more boldly about what you want to do.

There is a wide difference between those who have a vision of what a better future for their district, trust, unit, department, section, ward or practice would look like, and a set of objectives and targets for getting there, and those who have not lifted their head above their immediate concerns. These are the extremes; more commonly, managers will have objectives for improving and maintaining the work of their group, be it as wide as a district or just a small department, but lack the *vision* that is necessary for leadership. Setting objectives with target dates and reviewing their accomplishment are an essential part of management, but that is not leadership.

All managers can raise their sights, the first step towards developing a vision, if they ask themselves the 'Father Christmas' question; What would I most like Father Christmas to give me for my group? This can help you to think *what would be the ideal*. It helps also to try and picture what the ideal would look like, so that you can know when it has been achieved. Once you have made the ideal as concrete as you can, you can begin to work out how you can best move towards it. **It is important to believe that success is possible, while recognizing the obstacles that may need to be overcome.**

In attracting others to your vision, you need to identify the *values* that underpin it. This is best done with your staff, so that all can contribute and thus feel more committed to the values underlying the vision. This process can be done informally, but for authorities and trusts it can be useful to agree a written statement. Doing this helps to clarify common agreement on values, provides a reference point for future action and, if necessary, for criticizing action taken.

Spotlighting the way

Statements of value are words, and words can be powerful, but words unsupported by actions are meaningless, or worse because they encourage cynicism. **What you *do* matters more than what you say, because that shows what you really treat as important**. Hence it is no good saying that quality matters, and then spending little or none of your time on it. Tom Peters in *Thriving on Chaos*, has some powerful things to say about that:

> There is in fact no alternative to you acting as standard bearer for a dramatic strategic shift. You may if you are chief executive, appoint a 'representative' – a 'quality czar', for example. But beware. He or she can be no more than your point person, and never a true surrogate. There can be no substitute when it comes to the way the members of the organization assess your priorities and the seriousness of your intent. You are either 'on' the topic or you are not.[10]

> What matters is that everyone who works for and with you observes you embracing the topic with both arms – and your calendar. What they need to observe is your obvious, visible and dramatic, determination to batter down all barriers to understanding, and then implementation.[11]

By 'calendar', Peters means the time that you devote to the subject that you are saying is important.

You need to bear witness to the message that you want to put across by what you *say*, and what you *do*. Take opportunities to repeat the message, to use illustrations of what you mean, and (where you can) exemplify them in what you do. The Case Studies in Chapters 10 and 11 provide some examples.

All those who want to achieve a general change in attitudes and standards should remember that people respond to *symbols*; for example, a chief executive in an organization with strong status divisions could symbolize that he or she did not support them by giving up the reserved parking place. John Harvey-Jones, who was noted for his leadership as Chairman of ICI, is talking about symbolic actions when he says in his book on leadership:

> There is almost always something in a large organization that can be changed which will give very strong messages...In this process of change, small actions have a tremendous catalytic and change effect.[12]

Some of the DGMs in the Templeton study[13] also talked about their awareness in the early days in their new jobs of how quite small actions could symbolize the way things were going to change. One was making a night visit to the district general hospital, which was seen as the 'ivory tower' actually coming to see what staff had to put up with. Another was saying that a request for locks put in three months ago should be done the next day, and, when it was queried, that it was an order, not the start of an argument as to whose fault it was that it had not been done.

Problems of being a leader

We have been talking about leadership as it should be – the ideal – but there are difficulties inherent in being a leader.

EXCESSIVE EXPECTATIONS

People's expectations of what you can achieve may be unrealistic. This comes from the wish to believe that leadership will cure the ills that face an organization or even a society. The desire to attribute unrealistic power to leaders was shown in an American review of the meaning of leadership. It concluded that leadership is a romantic concept:[14] 'romantic' because of the belief that leaders can control the fates of the organizations in their charge. This belief is a double-edged sword for the leader, because it means that not only success, but also failure, are attributed (probably unduly) to the leader. However, the authors concluded that it is better for people in authority to believe that they can influence events, even if in doing so they exaggerate the extent to which they can control what happens, because this belief encourages them to initiate and to persist.

UNDUE IMPORTANCE ATTACHED TO YOUR REMARKS

People may pay too much attention to what you say, so that something you say casually may be noted and acted upon though you may not have wanted that. Most famously:

Who will free me from this turbulent priest?

(*Henry II*)

According to history books, said to have led to the murder of St Thomas Becket.

ISOLATION

As a leader you can easily become isolated, rather cut off from reality as it is experienced by those who work for you. This can make it harder to understand how others are feeling. It can also make you feel lonely. These are common dangers; fortunately less common are *folies de grandeur* – that is, an excessive belief in your own importance. Traditionally the court jester was a guard against this, as he had a licence to make fun of his master, but all leaders can benefit from having someone who will challenge them.

LACK OF CONFIDENCE

Leaders need to inspire confidence in others. This means that you may often need to appear more confident than you feel. It is a problem that usually gets less with age and experience in the job. It is common to feel more confident after some time in the job than when you are new to it.

Steps towards the ideal

These are described in the following chapters about leading in particular relationships, so only a few general guidelines are appropriate here:

1. **Do not be afraid to think of yourself as a leader** – the NHS needs leaders.
2. **You do not have to be superhuman to be a good leader, or even to be charismatic, but you must have a strong belief in what needs doing, a picture – even a vision** – of how you think the unit, department, ward, practice, or whatever you are responsible for managing should be.
3. **You need a willingness to convey that vision to others with enthusiasm and a visible personal commitment to its accomplishment.**
4. **You must be able to project yourself – the meek and the timid cannot be leaders – but many can learn to be more assertive when needed**.
5. It helps to have what Tom Peters and Nancy Austin[15] have called 'passion for excellence'.
6. **You should take a positive rather than a defeatist attitude to setbacks to your aims.**
7. **You should encourage others, but when you feel discouraged you may need to keep that to yourself**, though confiding in a friend or counsellor can be helpful.

Summary

1. The NHS needs leaders so do not be afraid to *think of yourself as a leader*. Good management and administration are necessary, too, but

it is leadership that will enable people to meet the many challenges facing the NHS.

2. Leaders have a *vision* of what they want to achieve. They point the way and make others enthusiastic about following it. They show clearly what they care about, and the values that underlie that.

3. Leaders are *demanding*: they set high goals. They make people feel proud of where they work. Above all, they make people feel important: they enable them to realize their potential.

4. There are *problems* about being a leader. People may expect too much. They may attach too much importance to what you say, even to chance remarks. You will have to cope with ambivalent attitudes to dependency. You may feel isolated at times. You may have to appear more confident than you feel.

5. Don't be put off. **You can be a leader if you have a strong belief in what needs doing and can convey that commitment to others. Remember that what you do matters more than what you say, because it shows what you really treat as important.**

PART II

LEADING IN
DIFFERENT RELATIONSHIPS

Introduction to part II

You should lead your staff, but you will often need to lead other people if you are to realize your ideal, your vision. The aim of Part II is to help you to do this. Each chapter is about a particular relationship and how you can lead in that relationship, starting with the most common, and usually the easiest, your staff. Each of the chapters in this part has the same three divisions:

1. The *ideal* to aim at.
2. The *difficulties* that commonly exist in achieving the ideal, and why they exist.
3. The *steps* that you can take to *move towards* the ideal.

You should use the suggested ideal to develop your own. Check to see which aspects of the ideal described you agree with, what you want to add, and what you want to delete.

WHY RELATIONSHIPS CAN BE DIFFICULT

There are five common reasons for friction between people:

1. **Their jobs require them to pursue different aims. These will make them look at problems from a different perspective**. A major example in the NHS is the difference between the clinician's aim of doing the best for the individual patient and the manager's need to consider the priorities for overall patient care within resource constraints.
2. **Differences in training and experience** develop distinctive values, ways of looking at the world and language – despite my best efforts, some of the words that I use in this book will be unfamiliar to some readers!
3. **Competition for scarce resources.**
4. **Differences in the power of different groups to influence decisions.**
5. **Personality clashes.**

The first and second reasons pose distinctive problems in the NHS because of the variety of separate professional careers. It is the tradition of distinctive fiefdoms – medicine, nursing and physiotherapy, to name

17

but a few – that makes leadership in general management posts such a challenge. There are changes, but the process is slow and painful. It is also challenging – and therefore interesting to good leaders – to learn how to lead those with other career backgrounds than their own. This does mean learning to *understand the way they see the world*. Chapter 4 on Leadership and Doctors discusses this, but it applies equally to understanding those from other backgrounds.

The third and fourth reasons for friction between people are more acute in the NHS than in many other organizations. The fifth can occur in any organization, but in the NHS it is, as Chapter 4 describes, most acute between consultants in the same hospitals.

When you are trying to make a relationship more effective, consider which of these causes is contributing to the problems. It is common – and all too easy – to attribute to personality, problems that have their main cause in differences in role or in background. Remember that a personality clash will stem at least in part from your own behaviour.

MANAGING YOUR RELATIONSHIPS

As a leader, you will want to manage your relationships so as to achieve your aims. First you will need to **develop a good network of contacts**. John Kotter highlighted the importance for managers of a network of contacts[1] that they can use to support the changes that they are trying to achieve, or to give them the information that they need. He showed how the general managers that he studied in the USA had a wide and diverse network of contacts, and took trouble to maintain them. Most managers have learnt to do so, but those who are still immersed in the professional aspects of their role often do not recognize how important a supportive network of contacts can be. If this is true of you, it is worth considering *whose support you need, and do not currently have*, to get your job done in the way that you want.

Next you should recognize the need to **manage the expectations** of those whom you are leading. You have expectations of what other people should do; they also have expectations of what you should do. John Machin, who with his students made many studies of the expectations that managers have of each other, showed that *expectations often do not match*.[2] People mistake what others expect of them and do not recognize – or even if they do, may not accept – other people's expectations. Once you know that a mismatch is likely, you will see the importance of trying to manage expectations so that as far as possible they do match. **You need to make clear to others what *you* expect of *them*, and seek to understand whether they accept these expectations. You can also try to influence what others *expect of you*.**

MANAGING CHANGE

Leadership means making changes, often radical changes – otherwise there would be no need for leadership! **Most changes affect people.** If the changes are to be successfully implemented, **people must be able and willing to implement them.** This is often hard, as one chief executive said:

> The problem is not knowing what to do, it is knowing how to get it done.

The first step is to recognize that **change needs to be managed.** Once you have decided what you want to achieve, you need to work out your strategy. What should you tackle first? You can get away with more when you are new in a job, as people then expect change – new brooms sweep clean. **Decide what you can do now, and what will take longer.** Often the delay will be because people do not see the need to change. Then you have a long process of **changing** their **attitudes**; that **is a key leadership task.** You need to 'sell' your ideas persuasively. You need to find and foster allies. When you want to achieve a particular change, think who is likely to be affected by it and whose support is most necessary.

Choose the *right time*. Some times are better than others for getting changes accepted because people are more open to accepting the need for change. Part of the art of managing change is recognizing when something has happened that makes people more willing to accept change. For example, an unexpected major budget deficit may make medical representatives more willing to consider changes to help to balance the books. An unfavourable report on the unit's work can also be a stimulus for accepting change.

There are a number of helpful guides to how to manage change, if you want to pursue this further.[3] An important message of all such guides is that change, if it is to be successfully implemented, must be managed – that is you must *develop a strategy* for how you are going to achieve the change, and particularly how you are going to *enlist the necessary support* for it.

Leading staff

'The essential thing in organizational leadership is that the leader's style pulls rather than pushes people on. A pull style of influence works by attracting and energizing people to an exciting view of the future. It motivates by identification, rather than through rewards and punishments.'

(Bennis and Nanus)[1]

In most jobs leading staff is a key aspect of your leadership. You can help to set the standards and values for their work. You can enable them to give of their best. You can grow future leaders.

Leading staff is the easiest form of leadership because you have more power to influence what happens. It is also easier because they are more likely to be looking for leadership than are the other people with whom you work. You have your own experience to draw on as a guide to what to do and what not to do, while remembering that your staff may differ from you.

The ideal

The ideal is stated in terms of your attitudes and actions:

1. **You will inspire, or at least enthuse, your immediate staff so that they share with you a common vision of what your group should be achieving,** whether the group for which you are responsible is as small as a few people or as large as a district or a trust.
2. **You will lead your staff towards a common goal that will override the potential disagreements about their relative roles.** This is particularly important if you are responsible for staff with very different roles.[2]
3. **You will enable your staff to give of their best towards the accomplishment of this shared goal.** The word 'empower' is useful because it highlights what a good leader can do to give staff the inspiration, energy, enthusiasm and the real responsibility for their work.

4. If you have a large staff **all will have seen and heard you, think that you are accessible to them** and, unless you are in charge of very many people, will also have **talked to you.** They will know what you stand for and feel proud of their leader. They may show this by telling stories about what you do that could be used as examples of good leadership.

5. **You will be aware of, and skilful in, the different facets of leadership**: leadership of *individuals* in one-to-one contacts; *group leadership* where you need to be like the conductor of an orchestra in encouraging those with different contributions to be heard adequately, but unlike the conductor in that you need not always be the one who is conducting a particular piece (project); and *symbolic leadership* as described in Chapter 1.

6. **You will develop future leaders by giving others opportunities to take the lead, and developing their confidence to do so.**

These are what you can contribute as a leader. Your staff also need a good manager. This book is about leadership rather than management, so only the attitudes and actions that shape your relationship with your staff are listed below. Management systems like the setting of objectives and review of performance, although useful management tools, are not part of a discussion of leadership.

You will need some other personal qualities as well:

7. **You will have the confidence in yourself that enables you to delegate, and the ability to assess the abilities of your staff and to develop them that enables you to do so with good results.**

8. **You really delegate, so that your staff know that they have full responsibility;** you delegate clearly, so that staff know what they are expected to do.

9. **You err on the side of being optimistic about what your staff can accomplish.**

10. **Your staff know that they can come to you for help and support if they have problems;** as John Harvey-Jones says:

> It is essential in a well-run company that in addition to the feeling of plenty of headroom and space to create and carry out one's job, there should be absolute confidence that those above will support one and that one can always look to them as a resource or as a help.[3]

It is just as essential that staff in the NHS should feel like that.

11. **Both you and your staff trust each other and feel supported by the other**, for bosses need support, too.

Difficulties in achieving the ideal

There are three potential sources of difficulty: *you, the situation and your staff*. Naturally most leaders are more conscious of the difficulties from the second and third of these, and are often unaware of the difficulties that stem from themselves.

THOSE THAT COME FROM YOU

1. There may be **personality defects**, but they are often ones that you may be able to overcome by learning through experience in challenging jobs;

(a) **A failure of nerve is one of the most serious, and the reason why many managers are not leaders.** Yet even those with leadership abilities may lose their nerve in face of difficulties and not hold to the course that they started on, without having made a judgement that this is the wisest thing to do.

(b) **A desire to be liked,** even to be seen as 'one of the boys' (or girls), is a weakness, because it can make you unwilling to take tough, and unpopular, decisions.

(c) **But do not glory in being unpopular** – leadership should not equate with martyrdom.

(d) **A pessimistic view of human character, so that you are reluctant to trust your staff to achieve.** If this trait is too strongly developed, you are unlikely to be a successful leader.

(e) **Inadequate energy, enthusiasm and drive, or ability for self-projection** to inspire, or at least to encourage, your staff.

2. There are difficulties that can come from the **way that you relate to your staff**:

(a) **Poor communication,** either in making clear your expectations or in your ability and interest in listening to what your staff have to say.

(b) **Failing adequately to see and treat your staff as individuals,** with different strengths and weaknesses and differences in the amount of direction, guidance and support that they need from you.

(c) **Paying too much attention to one group of staff and too little to another.** This does not mean that all should necessarily have the same amount of attention, but none should feel neglected or see you as inaccessible. This danger can exist in any job but is greatest if you are responsible for different types of staff.

3. Finally there are problems that come from a **failure to be on top of your job**:

(a) **Lack of clarity about goals** and the objectives needed to reach them.
(b) **Getting bogged down in operational problems**, so that you are too busy and preoccupied to give your staff the broader view that your position should provide.

FROM THE SITUATION

It is tempting to attach more blame to the situation than is justified but there are problems that constrain what the leader can do and therefore the leadership that he or she can provide for staff.

1. **The pressures on health services everywhere**, and the financial pressures upon the NHS, make management difficult and provide a challenging situation for leadership.
2. **The disruption to accustomed ways of working and the job insecurity brought by extensive organizational changes**. In any organization, major organizational changes necessarily bring a period of personal uncertainty and insecurity which distracts staff from wholehearted concentration on the work to be done.
3. **The culture of the NHS**, and the traditional belief that improvements can be achieved only with more resources, lowers the level of drive and optimism amongst staff.
4. **The difficulties of managing in a professional organization** where doctors, especially, see themselves primarily as independent professionals .
5. **It may be hard to recruit people of good calibre** in some occupations and the NHS salary levels may not be competitive for jobs that are in demand outside the Health Service. However, the Health Service does have an advantage over most other organizations in that contributing in whatever way to patient care can be seen to be worthwhile.

There are other situational difficulties for managers in the NHS such as political uncertainties and the extent of central intervention, but they are of less relevance to the leadership of staff than to some other relationships.

FROM STAFF

Complaining about poor staff is a temptation for many managers, so that you should always be chary of this explanation for leadership difficulties. However, some leaders are more fortunate than others. If they have been in the same job for some time part, at least, of that good fortune is likely to be of their own making.

A common difficulty is inheriting staff who are used to a quite differ-ent style, and find it hard to adapt. They may have been tightly con-trolled and have become unaccustomed to exercising initiative. You may find that some staff resent your getting the post, thinking that you are too young or come from an unsuitable background.

Steps towards the ideal

Do not be afraid to think of yourself as leading. It is right that a more democratic team approach has changed the ways in which managers relate to their staff, but there is a still a need for them to take a lead in times of change. This is most necessary in chief executive posts, but it is true at other levels too. Yet those who lead in practice may not think it right to think of themselves as a leader; for example, Bob Grindrod in Chapter 10 says:

> I would never say I lead my staff, I manage and develop them...I do not see it as leading, but as being human, it is helping others to grow. I feel somewhat uncomfortable at the idea of leading because my principle is that everyone is equal.

Ask yourself whether you are leading. You may be doing so because you are a natural leader, but you may have the capacity to lead yet have so far limited yourself to management, or even just to administration. So the first step is to assess whether you are *leading* your staff? The follow-ing points provide both a way of assessing how far you are leading, and guidance as to what you should do.

POINTING THE WAY

Leaders have followers: people who share a common vision and are enthusiastically pursuing it, so that will be one test of whether you are leading. Getting a common vision established will usually take time, so there may first be a very uphill 'selling' job to be done. The Case Studies in Chapters 10 and 11 show how some people have sought to get change accepted; the general guidelines in the introduction to Part II may also be helpful.

VISIBLE LEADERSHIP

Leaders should be seen because leadership is personal. You should be away from your desk much of the time. Visible leadership is especially important when there are major changes which make staff uncertain and insecure.

The NHS is becoming less bureaucratic. Yet some bureaucracy is inevitable in a politically sensitive public service but **you should, as far as possible, talk rather than write because it is much more personal and direct**. It also enables you to sense reactions, to respond and to be seen to do so. Sometimes you may want to confirm the action agreed in writing.

In relationships with staff in the NHS you have more choice of whether you talk or write than in some of the other relationships. Hence you can, and should, choose to talk – and even more *listen* – most of the time. One of the first generation district general managers, after he had been in the job for two years, said:

> I should have gone out and about for three months, looking really thoroughly at the organization. I should have talked to people in a semi-structured way, sharing their and my thoughts on what we should be going... I would recommend managers to do that even in the second generation of DGMs and beyond.

The DGMs who had done that felt that it had been worthwhile.

Your greatest power as a leader is the example that you set. The more your staff see you as their leader the more attention they will pay to what you do. Remember that people pay more attention to what you *do* than what you *say* – reread the section on the importance of symbols, pp. 11–12. In the case studies some of the individuals describe how they consciously seek to act in a way that they want their staff to follow, for example:

> You have to be aware that people will be watching you, so you need to lead by example. I try to behave in a mature, adult way to set an example.
>
> (Clare Dodgson, chief executive. Sunderland Health Authority)

> You have to think how your behaviour rubs off on people in all sorts of ways. Like walking the job and stopping to pick up litter rather than passing by. You need to be mindful of what you are saying and how you saying it at all times.
>
> (Nigel Clifford, chief executive, Glasgow Royal Infirmary University NHS Trust)

You should remember that some at least of your staff may not have had experience of the standards that you expect. You will need to show them by your own example what you mean. If, for example, you take quick action to remedy something that you are told is wrong, you are illustrating what you mean by responding quickly.

If you are heading a professional group you are a *role model* for the profession (a role model is someone whom others can use as a good example of how to act in that job, or how to act as a member of that profession). All leaders should be a model for relationships with staff so that theirs can learn – particularly if they are young – how to lead their own staff. The appreciation that such leadership can bring is illustrated by the following description of one district general manager:

> He leads from the top, he is the leader and he has made us leaders as well. He is leading by his own example because he puts so much into it and is thoroughly committed to the cause.

BALANCING TWO ASPECTS OF LEADERSHIP

Studies of leadership have shown that there are two contrasted aspects to the leader's job: *getting the work done* (that is, ensuring performance), and *showing consideration*. The importance of both of these should be known to you from your own experience of working for bosses.

Ideally a leader should be able to **keep both these aspects in balance**, so that the drive for performance does not ignore consideration, and the desire to be considerate does not weaken the drive for performance. If you are temperamentally much stronger on one than the other, it is important to recognize this, and to ensure that you have a senior member of staff who can balance you.

Both aspects of leadership are illustrated in the following quotations:

> He has a very personable, easy-going, friendly style but he is quite a taskmaster... everybody is under pressure to perform but that gets appreciation and recognition...If he gets the bit between his teeth he stays with it.

> He has not fallen into the trap of managers who have no mercy if deadlines for a whole range of tasks are not always met. The difference is between blind insistence and a flexible manager.

There can be a danger of having too high expectations of staff and of expressing frustration if they do not live up to them. One manager commenting on her chief executive said:

> There is a world of difference if somebody says to me: I am disappointed but I realize you are trying very hard or I am disappointed why don't you try harder?

That is an example where the drive for performance was seen to be out of balance with the need for consideration.

MAKE PEOPLE FEEL IMPORTANT

This, it may be remembered, was one of the leadership characteristics discussed in Chapter 1. It is more than showing consideration, though that is part of it. **Relate to the *person* first, before discussing the job.** This means, when you are visiting your staff, knowing them, taking an interest in what they are doing, and in what are their problems, and showing appreciation of good work. It is often good to do something out of the ordinary to mark your recognition of what they are contributing. Simple courtesies are important, too. We can learn from the French custom of greeting a shop assistant before asking for what is wanted, as a recognition of her as a person.

ADAPT TO INDIVIDUALS

You need to do this in the way that you relate to different staff. Some need more encouragement than others; some need more guidance; some are easily hurt, and so on.

You also need to adapt in the sense that John Harvey-Jones describes:

> Companies in the past, have tended to expect that their employees should conform to the wishes of the company. This is becoming less and less practical as a philosophy of operation, and I believe absolutely that in the future it will be the company that conforms to the individual that attracts and motivates the best people. Companies will have to be more flexible in their demands, to accommodate more and more the individuals' different hopes, wishes and ambitions.[4]

If this is true for companies, who have had much greater flexibility in rewarding their staff, it should be even more true for the NHS. Within the bureaucratic constraints, you will have some opportunities to take account of individual differences. Doing so is one way of showing that you see people as individuals.

DEVELOP LEADERS

One of your most important tasks is to develop leaders of the future. You can do much to encourage others to have the confidence to be leaders, as some of the young leaders in Chapter 10 testify. You can do much, too, to develop your staff by giving them challenging tasks that match their abilities, but remaining supportively in the background.

Leaders have followers but they should also help them to grow into leaders: 'followers' in the sense of being attracted to the leader's sense of purpose, but not in being dominated by the leader's personality.

ENCOURAGE CHALLENGE

One of the dangers of being a leader, particularly at the top of your particular pyramid, is that you may become complacent, or just blinkered. Hence you should encourage your staff to *challenge you*. John Harvey-Jones describes this challenging role as follows:

> What we are looking for is what I call constructive no-men...who will tell us what I or the company should be doing differently.[5]

It is often hard to get your staff to challenge you, since they may be hesitant to do so, particularly if you have a forceful personality. Taking your immediate staff away for a day or two is a method that many general managers have found helps to encourage a more open and searching discussion of major policy issues and of the problems of working together. More junior leaders who are not in a position to do that can still have a short away time for the same purpose – even if 'away' is only in a conference room – but make clear it is not a normal committee or consultative meeting.

Reread the difficulties that may come from your own behaviour that were described earlier in the chapter. Try to get some honest feedback about which of these apply to you.

Finally, use your sense of humour and show that work can be fun, at least some of the time.

Summary

1. Leadership of staff is the easiest form of leadership, but carries a great responsibility. The key ideal is that *you will inspire your staff to share a common vision of what you should be achieving.* You will enable your staff to give of their best. You will grow future leaders.
2. There are three potential sources of difficulty; *you, the situation and the staff themselves.* Beware of blaming the last two and not recognizing the difficulties that *you* may cause.
3. The steps that you can take towards the ideal are first to ask yourself whether you are *leading* or only directing and monitoring your staff? Check how far you *are* leading by the extent to which you do the following:

- seek to get agreement on a *common vision and values;*
- set a *visible example*: be seen and known;
- set *high standards of performance* for yourself and others;
- balance this with *consideration for your staff;*

- make people *feel important*;
- adapt to *individuals' needs and wishes*;
- develop your staff by *stretching them*, but be supportively in the background;
- encourage your staff to challenge you; seek to get *honest feedback*.

CHAPTER 3

Leadership and nurses

'listening (especially to those at the front) remains the truest signal that "I take you seriously"'.

(Tom Peters)[1]

'The undervaluing of nursing is the single largest problem facing the health service.'

(Howard Davies, when he was head of the Audit Commission)

The ideal to be aimed at in the leadership of, and by, nurses, midwives and health visitors must take account of the ways in which nursing (for convenience 'nursing' is used from now on to include midwives and health visitors) differs from other occupations in the NHS or in private health care. It must also take account of what should be supported and maintained and what it is desirable to try to change. Above all it must take account of the major changes that are affecting nursing and nurses

The word 'leadership' is used in this chapter as it is described in Chapter 1, so is wider than merely professional leadership. It embraces leadership of and by nurses at all levels. It includes, too, nurses in their broader managerial and corporate role.

The characteristics of nursing that affect the leadership task, and which often make it more difficult, are:

1. The professional concerns of maintaining a code of conduct and of establishing and monitoring standards, characteristics of all professions but of particular importance for a large group of staff working in direct patient care. The monitoring is made more complex by recruiting nurses of varying abilities from a wide cross-section of the community.
2. The large size and diversity of the nursing staff.
3. Ninety per cent of nurses are female but there is a disproportionate number of men in higher grades – about forty per cent in the highest grades.[2]
4. Racial inequality in nursing is widespread and deep-seated.[3]

5. A young and predominantly short-term workforce in the acute hospital service.
6. The traditional subordinacy of the nurse, in many types of nursing, to the doctor, although this is changing.
7. The continuous provision of nursing care over the 24 hours.
8. The stressful nature of the work.

IMPACT OF THE REORGANIZATIONS ON NURSING

The leadership task is also influenced by the many changes to the NHS taking place since 1984 that have affected the jobs and status of nurses and particularly of senior nurses.

There are both *increased opportunities for, and threats to, nurses from the changes introduced since the late 1980s*. In the early stages of the changes nurses expressed two fears about their status being undermined. One was that nurses' knowledge was not being taken adequately into account in managerial decision making. This fear centred on provision for nursing advice to the district general manager and the district health authority.[4] The other main anxiety was about nursing management and the belief that nurses should be led by nurses.

The changes since *Working for Patients* have aroused fresh concerns. One is whether nursing experience is sufficiently taken into account in purchasing. Another has come from the major reduction in the regional nursing function in the reorganization of regions: one regional nursing adviser has replaced a sizeable regional nursing directorate.

A more general concern was shown in the 1994 campaign, the Right to Nurse: 'the right to give the high quality patient care that nurses are capable of and are committed to'.[5] This was launched by the Royal College of Nursing and the Nursing Standard. Announcing the campaign, Christine Hancock, the RCN's general secretary said:

> For many nurses today, their working environment seems like an obstacle course, with hurdles to good care confronting them at every turn.[6]

There has also been, for the first time, the threat of redundancy and of it being difficult to find a nursing job of equivalent grade. The size of the nursing budget means that top management in trusts are looking for ways of reducing it. This has meant both cuts in the numbers of nurses and changes to the skill mix. Nursing unemployment has remained low, but more are now employed – as is a general trend in organizations – on a short-term contract, temporarily or via an agency.

Despite all these concerns, it should be remembered that nurses have also gained in a number of ways from the changes that have been taking place in the delivery of care. This is most marked in primary care where nurses play a larger and expanding role. The number of nurses working in primary care has also increased markedly and so has the importance attached to their role.[7]

In trusts there are opportunities for nurses to play a wider role as members of management teams at different levels. There are also opportunities to move to general management. The fact that a nurse executive must be a member of the acute and mental health trust boards has restored the position that existed before the introduction of general management.

Some nurses have realized that the changes since the introduction of general management have created many new opportunities for nurses. As Elizabeth McElkerney put it in an article written from a hospital perspective:

> Nurses are beginning to accept that the advent of Griffiths and the concept of general management is all about empowering nurses to use their width of management experience to take them into positions of power.[8]

In the early days of purchasing, fears that there was an inadequate nursing contribution led to an NHSME commissioned study in 1992. The report by the King's Fund College[9] suggested that there are a number of areas where nurses could make an important and distinctive contribution to purchasing. One, which also applies to management in trusts, is their ability to speak several languages: that of doctors, nurses, managers and lay people. This can help them to act as bridges between different points of view. 'Understanding the business' was described as another nursing contribution, particularly in relation to the setting and auditing of clinical standards.

Since that 1992 report, which was written in the early days of purchasing, the NHSE produced a report in 1994 on the role that nurses could play in purchasing,[10] which carried on its front an endorsement by Dr Brian Mawhinney, Minister for Health:

> I wish to see the new system informed and improved by the general input and the specific experience of nurses. I want you to be at the forefront in the development of purchasing as well as clinical and professional leadership. It is essential that purchasers seek expert nursing advice.

Many other changes also affect the ideal for nursing leadership. There are the changes in nurse education resulting from Project 2000 and in the skill mix of nurses. Nurses have been developing their clinical base so that they can undertake work that was previously done by doctors.

There are changes in the organization of community care, in the changing nature of disease and increasing use of technology, the pressures brought by shorter stays in hospital and by more demanding patients.

All these changes have made front-line nurses anxious, as the 'Right to Nurse' campaign recognized. A study in 1992 of three first-wave community trusts found a contrast between managers and nurses. Generally, managers thought they could use changes for their own ends, whereas nurses saw change as threatening.[11] In 1994, Professor Joan Higgins argued that the reforms had divided people into doers, who have power, influence and budgets and who have welcomed the challenge of the changes, and the done-to. She warned:

> Unless the enthusiastic doers begin to address the problems of uncertainty, insecurity and cynicism experienced by many of the done-to during periods of rapid change, the NHS reforms may do lasting damage to the fabric of the service and to those who work in it.[12]

The ideal

Some ideals should be common to all leaders, whatever their career background, who are in charge of nurses. These are in addition to the ideals discussed in Chapter 2 about leadership and staff:

1. **The quality of care, in all its aspects, receives continued and critical attention.**
   Nurses are concerned about the *effectiveness* of what they do. This concern shows itself in a critical approach to nursing methods that is supportive of research into nursing practice and of the implementation of research findings about the best practice.

2. **Nurses respect the individuality of their patients including their values and beliefs.**
   This means working in partnership with them as 'A Vision for the Future: The Nursing, Midwifery and Health Visiting Contribution to Health and Health Care', published by the NHSME in 1993, put it: 'the future imperative' is 'to work in partnership with other professionals, users of services and their carers'.[13]

3. **Senior nurses exemplify good nursing practices and attitudes.**

4. **Senior nurses' attitudes to less experienced nurses:**
   Senior nurses understand the motivations and problems of junior nurses, and how these may have changed from when they started in

nursing. They also recognize the additional uncertainties and anxieties that nurses may feel in times of organizational change. They create a climate in which nurses feel that they can complain about errors and mismanagement without being labelled as 'trouble-makers'. The importance of encouraging *whistle blowing* was recognized in the early 1990s as a result of offical inquiries into disasters and gross misconduct in various organizations. In 1993 a free legal advice centre, Public Concern at Work, was established.

5. **Nurses' ability to be effectively assertive:**
   Nurses have the ability and the confidence to express their views cogently in meetings with managers and doctors.

6. **Development and promotion of nurses:**
   Individual performance review (IPR) highlights nurses with abilities for promotion who should then be given opportunities for development.
   (a) Nurses are encouraged to develop their professional and leadership knowledge and understanding, so that they can play their full part in corporate management.
   (b) Wider career opportunities are available to nurses both within nursing and in general management.
   (c) Ambitious nurses recognize the varied opportunities available.
   (d) Nurses have the confidence to go for promotion and to take on managerial roles.

7. **Equality of opportunities:**
   That good progress is made in reducing sexual and racial discrimination with the aim of working towards their elimination.

8. **Staffing:**
   There are the numbers and kinds of nurses that are needed for different services, and these are used effectively. This ideal has three aspects: assessing staffing needs, using staff effectively and recruiting and retaining nurses.

9. **Nurses in primary care who have different qualifications work well together.**

There is an additional ideal, that managers with a non-nursing background should aim at:

10. **Nursing experience is adequately represented in all decision-making because it will ultimately affect patient care.**

Difficulties in achieving the ideal

The difficulties stem in part from the attitudes of others towards nurses, and in part from those of *nurses themselves* which contribute to the formation of others' attitudes. The common *constraint of finance* also limits some – but by no means all – of the actions that can be taken towards achieving the ideal.

Difficulties can be divided into those stemming from the changes in nurses' roles in the later 1980s and in the 1990s and other (potentially longer-term) difficulties. The latter are discussed first because of their longer-term significance.

NURSING ATTITUDES

There have been major changes in the last few years which have reduced many of the previous problems. The traditionally strong nursing hierarchy, which emphasized control and discouraged assertiveness has changed. The hierarchy in hospitals is flatter than before and nurses much sooner play a dual role of nursing and management.

The traditional subordinacy of nurses to doctors lingers in more old-fashioned places, but elsewhere nurses are recognized as equally important team members. Nurse-led services are also increasing. Now nurses may also act as bridges between managers and doctors as they understand the clinical aspects of problems and are more ready to accept the need for management.

But problems remain, in part at least, because most nurses are *women*, who have only recently been encouraged to assert themselves. Assertiveness is now recognized as a necessary aspect of leadership but **nurses have often lacked assertive skills. They have tended to feel aggrieved, but to lack the self-confidence and the skills to press for their grievances to be remedied**. Doing so will be more difficult where they work in a macho climate.

Problems too remain from the parochialism and jealousies that easily develop between separate but related specialities within a broader profession. This has been a particular danger in primary care because of the existence of different forms of education and qualifications. These problems should be reduced by the introduction of a common curriculum.

David Benton, who won the 1993 leadership in nursing award sponsored by Ashridge Management College, suggests that:

> The experiences, skills and knowledge that nurses can bring to the current health agenda are limited only by the reluctance they have to explore the unknown.[14]

NURSING EDUCATION AND TRAINING

Until recently nursing education in the UK emphasized practical skills. It did not develop powers of logical argument in speech or on paper, nor did it encourage a respect for the value of research into the best methods of nursing. The emphasis on training in, and adherence to, procedures as the way of ensuring that standards are maintained did not encourage a questioning approach, or much attention to the development of standards.

The 1994 NHSE report on nurses' contribution to purchasing said that nurses felt constrained by the lack of specific education and training for purchasing, since the skills are so different from those used in a provider unit.[15]

ATTITUDES OF MANAGERS TO NURSES

Managers have tended – and still tend – to underrate the contribution of the nursing viewpoint to decision-making. It is noteworthy that in the reports of the Templeton tracer study of district general managers, we were unable to write one on the DGM and nursing because it was a subject that was rarely mentioned by most of the twenty DGMs studied. In the earlier study of district administrators[16] they were often dismissive of the district nursing officer, though for some this may have been a reflection of their lack of interest in patient and service issues in general. These studies are now old, but the problem often remains. Although some nurses are playing a bigger role in hospital management and in primary care, others have lost out, particularly in purchasing and in the regions.

Managers' attitudes to nurses are probably due in part to the inadequate ability of nurses, at least in the past, to express their views cogently. This is gradually changing with changes in nurses' education and with the number of nurses taking MBAs and other management qualifications.

Another reason why nurses' views may get less attention than doctors is that they are less powerful and less 'difficult' than doctors, so that their views do not compel managers' attention in the way that doctors are able to do.

NEW AND POTENTIAL PROBLEMS

Many problems change over time and these changes may not be anticipated because of unforeseen changes in health care or in the economy. A major fear in the 1980s was of a *shortage of nurses*, but by the mid-1990s this was only for some specialities. Christine Hancock predicted shortages in paediatric and community psychiatric nurses unless urgent action was taken to plan sufficient student intake.[17]

For general nurses the problem had unexpectedly *changed to a shortage of jobs* in hospitals. Three reasons probably explain this dramatic change. One is the radical changes in hospital care. Two was the recession, and the third is the pressure on trusts to make efficiency gains.

The growth in the number of practice nurses raises special problems because they can easily feel isolated. A 1992 survey of practice nurses in Barking and Havering FHSA concluded that 'serious issues concerning training, competency indemnity and audit of work have to be addressed if practice nurses are to take their rightful place in the primary care team.'[18]

There are also problems that come from uncertainties, particularly in purchasing, as to what role nurses can play. The NHSE report, 'Building a stronger team: the nursing contribution to purchasing', reported that one of the constraints was that: 'many are still "feeling their way" through a period of evolution and organisational change'.[19]

Nursing turnover used to be a serious problem, but with greater uncertainties in the labour market it has declined markedly. Only four per cent of nurses left NHS employment in 1993.[20] However, it is still worth any trust examining its turnover rates. These vary markedly by age and length of service.

Another way in which nurses, like other staff, register concern about their working conditions is by absence. Nurse absence is high and costly: so it should be monitored regularly, compared with similar trusts, and attempts made to discover the reasons for it and what can be done to reduce it.[21]

It is the fears and uncertainties caused by the extensive changes and reorganizations that have affected nurses, as well as other staff, that is the major problem. It is likely to be only the most energetic and self-confident who focus on the new opportunities that have been created for them and for their careers. The Right to Nurse campaign, mentioned earlier, is indicative of a widespread problem of nursing morale.

Steps towards the ideal

The ideal for nurses can be summed up as: ensuring that the knowledge and experience of nurses is used most effectively in the delivery of care **and** in the strategies for providing patient-relevant and responsive care. **There is a need for leadership that encourages nurses** to develop a more entrepreneurial approach to achieving what they see to be important.

FOR SENIOR NURSES

There are four areas where senior nurses should be exercising leadership: as a member of the corporate executive; as leader of the nursing profession; in influencing clinical practice; and in staff development.

Member of the Corporate Executive

> Until nurses truly value their contribution to the wider corporate agenda, and ensure that they not only articulate their professional opinions confidently, but also understand the political subtleties of how other key players manoeuvre, then their ability to negotiate and exert real influence on the future of health care will remain limited.
>
> (Heather-Jane Sears, 1994)

> When you try to stay within your own camp and argue your own corner you lose out. When you can start to see the bigger picture you can operate in a managerial arena. Many nurses are not very good at this, perhaps because they do not have the confidence. Many do not see that you can contribute outside the nursing function. Nurses have often been their own worst enemies because they always argued a parochial case.
>
> (Senior manager with a nursing background)

In NHS Trusts, the executive nurse is leader of much the largest staff group and therefore has a major contribution to make to many corporate discussions. To do so effectively requires a good understanding of broader management problems and with that, an ability to see nursing as part of corporate management.

Leader of the Nursing Staff

An important aspect of being a leader is acting as a *role model*, that is as an example to staff both of how to behave and of career possibilities – hence the value for young women of a female role model in a senior job. The value of a role model is true at each level from staff nurse for student nurses up to the most senior manager. Heather-Jane Sears, when a hospital manager and one of the young leaders described in Case Study 5a of Chapter 11, illustrated some of the different ways in which a nurse manager can be a role model of good practice. She said:

> I was more of a role model when I was a ward sister than I am now as hospital manager because then I was constantly being watched and teaching.

but she also illustrated various ways in which she was currently a role model:

> Every time I walk down to a ward I do nursing duties and then I am a role model. For example in lifting a patient, I automatically shift into a professional role model: you are teaching all the time and trying to pull up the standard of excellence in the hospital.

> I am a role model in a different way from when I was a sister, I am now a role model managerially: getting people to examine their practices by showing the value of research-based practice rather than by doing things because we had always done them that way.

> I am a role model to my staff about professional attitudes and confidentiality. I talk to patients and their relatives often in front of the staff. When interviewing for staff, I always have a staff nurse there as well for them to learn.

> I am also a role model for time management, as I have to structure my time carefully and pack a lot into my day. I often talk to staff about doing the same: about priorities, planning, thinking before you rush in and do. It is easy in nursing and domestic work, when you are busy, to chase your tail!

If nurses are to be leaders outside their own nursing staff they have to be heard, so learn to *express yourself more cogently* if you feel that your views do not get sufficient attention. Take, if necessary in your own time and at your own expense, courses in effective speaking and writing, interdisciplinary negotiating and committee skills and possibly also in assertiveness.

> In presenting your case stick to the issue, do not respond to undercurrents of prejudice to ward nurses, or to tensions between the trust and the purchasers, but work diplomatically towards what you want.
>
> (advice given by one senior nurse)

Influencing Nursing Practice

Agree the *overall philosophy* that should underly all nursing policies and practice. The executive nurse with her/his nursing colleagues can give a lead to nurses by agreeing a nursing philosophy for the trust, and by making sure that it is widely known.

The establishment and maintenance of high standards of care is an essential role of nurse leaders at all levels, but particularly that of the ward sister and her equivalents in the community. Those managers who do not have a nursing background will need to enlist the interest and help of their nursing colleagues in doing so. **A system of regular reporting on performance against measurable standards is necessary if attention to quality of care is not to be a number of disconnected and short-lived efforts at improvement**.

A high quality of care means not only establishing standards and monitoring that they are being maintained but also looking for ways of *improving* them. A good nursing network will enable you to compare practice as one way of finding what others are doing to improve the standards of care. Such sharing was one of the twelve useful targets put forward by the NHSME in 1993 as practical means of ensuring that nurses, midwives and health visitors play their full part in the policy changes in the NHS.[22]

Leaders should challenge accepted practice, and encourage their staff to do so too. Nurses need to learn to think *critically* about what they do. It takes time for nurses both to develop the courage to criticize their own practice and to make changes. Unless they are encouraged and supported in doing so, they simply become defensive. Recent developments with reflective practice in nursing have helped to develop critical self-assessment, enabling practitioners to evaluate and develop their professional practice, and make more sense of challenging clinical situations.[23]

A good example of a new approach to an old problem is Pam Hibbs's research into pressure sores. She found that to prevent pressure sores you must implement a programme of preventive action for particular categories of patients within an hour of their admission to hospital.[24] Pressure sores, in addition to the discomfort to the patient, mean longer in hospital and greater cost. She developed a system for getting data to monitor pressure sores. Since then the Department of Health issued 'Pressure Sores, a Key Quality Indicator', and commissioned Touche Ross, management consultants, to assess the costs of prevention which illustrated that achieving quality can be expensive.[25]

Quality of care includes other patient services as well as nursing. The 'hotel' aspects of patient care – catering, cleaning and laundry may be contracted out. Whether they are or not, senior nurses should try to ensure that the nursing philosophy is implemented and that the patient is treated like a *customer who has a right to expect good service*. The latter can require a change of attitude that will not happen of its own accord.

See the patient as a customer. Some clinicians, whether nurses or doctors, dislike the idea of patients as customers which they see as alien to their view of professional service. This is understandable. It is a view that can come from the best motives of service and of responsibility to the individual, where the analogy of treating a patient like a relative is seen as more appropriate. However, it is a view that can also come from a feeling of superiority. *If you shy at the word 'customer', ask yourself whether this is because you prefer to think of the patient as dependent upon* *you?* The idea of a patient as a client or customer with the right both to good service in all its aspects and to be critical of any failings in that service is less comfortable than that of a dependent patient who ought to be grateful.

Recognize the patient's right of choice. This ideal applies to both doctors and nurses, whose philosophy towards the patient needs to develop together. Statements of nursing philosophy now stress the value of ensuring that patients have *choice* rather than being subject to what nurses think is best for them, or what is most convenient for the nurses. Ideally such a value statement should be linked to a companion one by *doctors* in the same trust.

There are some advantages for nurses as well as for patients in such a recognition, as Catherine McLoughlin, when district general manager (DGM) of Haringey Health Authority, pointed out when she contrasted the responsibility that patients take – and are expected to take – for themselves before admission to hospital and after their discharge, with the dependence on staff while they are in hospital.[26] She said:

> I strongly believe that we must change our management of individual care to one which allows them to remain responsible for themselves and the activities which occur to them during their stay in hospital. I believe that is in the individual patient's interest, I also believe that it would reduce the workload being undertaken by nursing staff, there-fore, would reduce the stress which they feel.

Staffing and Development

Recruit and retain nurses. The relationship between you and the nursing staff will be one of the factors that determine how many of the nursing recruits stay, and for how long. You should ensure that you are known by the nurses, and that you are seen to be *accessible to, and supportive of,* them.

Revans showed in the 1960s how much could be learnt by studies of nursing attitudes. However, attitude surveys are useful only if they are followed up. This was the central message of the Revans approach. He wanted hospital staff to diagnose their own organizational problems and seek to solve them themselves in a more open way than was usual in hospitals.[27] His advice remains apposite 30 years later.

Use nurses effectively. Ward managers should be encouraged to think about the *effective use of their time, and that of their staff* by, for example, comparing staff usage in their own ward with that in other wards and by benchmarking with other hospitals. Such comparisons are one of the ways in which the provision of better information can be used to help clinicians, whether doctors or nurses, to compare what they do with their peers as a way of considering the effectiveness with which they work.

Nurses, like other staff, need to be helped and encouraged to develop themselves. They – especially the women – may need more encouragement than most to be confident in their abilities and in their aspirations. Encouraging them to acquire additional clinical qualifications is relatively easy; more difficult is the transition from a nurse manager still directly involved in nursing to that of a manager with wider responsibilities. Individuals may need help in deciding whether they really want to make that transition, with the different attitudes that it requires. They will also need training to help them to compete successfully with those from other career backgrounds. **You should encourage them to think positively and proactively about the wider career opportunities now open to them**.

You should seek to *spot leadership talent early*, so that it can be developed. This can be done only if you meet nurses in situations where they are not too nervous to speak up. Visiting can provide an opportunity for talking to staff, if you have the skill to do that informally. Sometimes, at least, you should do your homework first by asking managers about their abler staff and noting who are getting extra qualifications or showing leadership in some way, and then making a point of talking to them. Asking for volunteers for particular projects, like organizing an open day or study event, is yet another way of trying to find who are the people who may have promotion potential.

Nurses should be encouraged to *develop specialist knowledge* of particular areas. Trusts can benefit from having nurses with specialist knowledge, which can range from subjects like child abuse to the prevention of pressure sores. They can lead others in their area of specialist knowledge by highlighting the need for a statement of policy from the trust or even from local purchasers, by contributing their expertise to discussions of procedures and by teaching others to improve their practice. However, it is important that greater specialization in nursing is not at the expense of a holistic view of the patient.

Help your staff to *learn to express themselves well*, both in speaking and writing.

FOR PRIMARY CARE NURSES

The emphasis on care in the community with its shift from hospital-based nursing means that there is a much larger role for nurses in primary care. Nurses are also taking on more responsibility than before both as members of practice teams and in autonomous roles which are breaching many of the boundaries that have traditionally constrained nurses. Similar developments in the nursing role are also taking place in the acute sector.

FOR CHIEF EXECUTIVES

Recognize that nurse managers have experience that is very relevant to decisions about patient care. Ensure that they are *included* in decision-making and, if necessary, help them to make that contribution.

A nursing philosophy should be part of the trust's planning of services. For example, a principle of not making patients dependent is relevant to decisions about how care should be provided. Raise the question of whether a parallel statement of philosophy should also be drawn up by the doctors working in the trust.

Do not adopt the popular stereotype of the nurse as the handmaiden of the doctor – for example, *do not overvalue doctors' views compared to nurses'*, nor praise their contribution at the expense of other contributors. You may be tempted to do the latter if you are nervous of doctors' power and are seeking to placate them. **More usually it will be the nurses who need reassurance that you are listening to what they say**.

Consider allocating small sums of money to *encourage* and *reward good care*.

FOR CHAIRS AND BOARD MEMBERS

Encourage the senior nurses to develop a statement of the trust's nursing philosophy, if they have not already done so, for discussion at a board meeting. Seek to ensure that this philosophy is *known* and *understood* by nurses throughout the trust.

Discover what figures are provided to other trusts to check that you are being given **the most appropriate information** for you to judge the standard of care provided in your own trust.

Recognize the importance of a high nursing morale, and do what you can to show your appreciation of nurses' work.

Consider the ideals listed at the start of the chapter and ask for a statement of nursing objectives, compare them with the suggested ideals to see if there are any major omissions that you should query. Ask for an occasional review of progress towards the objectives.

Summary

1. Nurses and nursing are beginning to receive the critical, but supportive, attention that will be essential in the future.
2. Leadership of, and by, nurses is wider than professional leadership. It embraces all aspects of leadership of nurses, whether by nurses or by managers from other backgrounds. The leadership of nurses must take account of the many distinctive characteristics of nursing and of the changes affecting nursing. It also embraces the contribution that nurses should be making to corporate management.

3. There are *different kinds of ideal* to aim at:

- the continued and critical attention to quality of care;
- the effective use of nurses;
- high nursing morale;
- effective training and career development;
- effective contribution by nurses to decisions about patient care and resource management.

4. Difficulties in achieving the ideal come from the attitudes of others towards nurses, from nurses themselves and from difficulties caused by reorganizations.
5. Steps towards the ideal suggested for senior nurse managers fall into four groups:

(a) *Member of the corporate executive*
- see nursing as part of corporate management;
- develop an understanding of broader management issues.

(b) *Leader of nursing staff*
- act as a role model;
- speak up effectively for nurses, and help your staff to learn to do so too.

(c) *Influencing nursing practice*
- agree nursing philosophy;
- establish and maintain high standards of care;
- challenge accepted practice and encourage others to do so too;
- see the patient as having a right to good service in all its aspects;
- recognize patients' right of choice.

(d) *staffing and development*
- be active in recruiting and retaining nurses;
- be accessible to, and supportive of, nurses;
- use nurses effectively;
- help and encourage nurses to develop themselves;
- encourage a positive approach to wider career opportunities.

The suggestions for chief executive, for the chair and board members are brief enough not to need summarizing. Use the account of the ideal as a way of judging what may need attention. The key message is that in the quotations at the head of this chapter: often too little attention is paid to nursing views, in part because some nurses are still not very good at expressing themselves.

CHAPTER 4

Leadership and doctors

'The doctors lead the technology, and therefore the pattern of service. Unless managers get the doctors with them, everything else is just window-dressing. That is where you have got to get change.'

(District General Manager in the Templeton study)

The quotation is still true today and will remain so because it highlights a key leadership task. This is to enlist doctors' cooperation in the provision of effective and efficient health care. It is a task that must not be avoided by those who should be seeking to influence doctors.

What has changed since the late 1980s, when the first edition of this book was written, is that there are many new opportunities for doctors to lead outside the traditional clinical ones. There is also a new challenge to managers to seek to influence GPs.

Many more doctors are involved in management and thus in the leadership task of influencing other doctors and in helping to shape the organization's strategy. An even greater change is the increasing leadership role in general practice. GPs are far more influential than they used to be. So they have an opportunity to exercise leadership by participating in groupings of GPs, and, at the time of writing, of GPFs as purchasers, as well as by contributing to the health authority's strategy. These wider leadership opportunities also mean that there is more need for leadership in the larger practices since the partners should agree on a strategy. Some of the new leadership opportunities for doctors are illustrated in the case studies in Chapter 11.

Yet another change for doctors is the continuing shift away from an authoritarian approach. Now many more staff expect to be treated as fellow members of a team rather than as subordinates.

The leadership task is greater and more complex in large organizations, so much of the discussion is about hospital doctors.

The ideal

The ideal attitudes and actions for doctors are listed first, because it is these ideals that leaders, whatever their backgound, should be seeking to achieve. These ideals do not include the central medical ideals about patient care, because they are about doctors as members of an organization.

DOCTORS

Doctors will:
  1. **Understand the need for management.**

(a) Recognize that resources need managing and are always bound to be limited, so that choices have to be made about service priorities.
(b) Recognize that resources can be used with varying degrees of effectiveness and be active in considering how to use them most effectively.

  2. **Be willing to contribute to management.**
     Realize that if they are not willing to give the time to consider managerial problems, and to share in the taking of difficult resource decisions, they are leaving this task to managers without medical backgrounds, and may not like the results.
  3. **Realize the value of learning about management.**
  4. **Recognize that there are other views than the medical of what health policy and health improvement should look like.**
  5. **Place concern for patient care above professional loyalty.**
     So be willing to tackle problems arising from failings of individual doctors' performance whatever the cause.
  6. **Recognize a corporate responsibility for patient care.**
     Hence in bidding for resources accept that others may have a greater need for them.
  7. **Be active in reviewing their own performance.**

(a) Seek to establish quantitative and qualitative measures of outcomes.
(b) Compare their performance with that of their peers and seek to improve.
(c) Support those doctors who take the lead in peer review.

  8. **Show appreciation of the contribution to patient care of nurses, paramedics, and other staff, behave courteously towards them and treat them as fellow members of a team.**
  9. **Recognize and adjust to the changing roles of other professions,** for example, psychologists and biochemists.
  10. **Treat patients as intelligent individuals.**
      Be willing to discuss treatment options and their implications with them.

The ideals described below are those that leaders should pursue and seek to get accepted by all managers whatever their professional background.

MANAGERS

Managers will:
1. **Be resiliently proactive in trying to achieve the ideals listed above**. Avoid the dangers of hand wringing about medical attitudes and of abdicating any responsibility for the pursuit of these ideals.
2. **Be seen as the trusted arbitrator between different medical interests**.
3. **Express the corporate values and goals in a way that makes sense to doctors**.
4. **Seek to create an environment in which professionals can give of their best**.
5. **Recognize the stress of doctors' jobs and try to be as helpful as possible**.
6. **Seek to ensure that the chair, chief executive and medical director adopt a common approach in their discussions with doctors**.

DOCTORS AND MANAGERS

There is one ideal that should apply to both doctors and managers.

Recognize and understand the different roles that doctors and managers have to play in the NHS and the attitudes that come both from that and from differences in training.

TRUST CHAIRS

The chair will:
1. **Recognize that the chair's status helps in negotiations with doctors and therefore be willing to devote the necessary time**.
2. **Be supportive of and available to doctors' representatives and listen to their concerns but recognize that their arguments may be one-sided**.
3. **Take care really to understand the issue that is arousing doctors' ire, so as not to make injudicious comments**.
4. **Recognize the need to enlist doctors' cooperation and avoid remarks and actions that may stimulate a collective vote of no confidence – as has happened occasionally**.
5. **Agree – and keep to – the strategy for pursuing changes that move nearer to the ideal**.

Authority chairs also need to understand the views of medical directors and of GPs. They should also recognize the importance of promoting evidence based medicine.

Difficulties in reaching the ideal

RELATIONSHIPS BETWEEN DOCTORS AND MANAGERS

The Introduction to Part II gave five possible *reasons for the difficulties that leaders may have in seeking to influence others*: differences in roles, differences in training and experience, competition for scarce resources, differences in relative power, and particular personality problems. All are reasons why the relationship between doctors and managers so often causes problems for the managers.

Differences in Role
Doctors' primary role is to treat individual patients. They may play other roles as well: teaching, researching, fund raising, managing their department or firm, and serving on national medical councils. Some may also spend part of their time in a management role. But in their primary role, their responsibility is to the individual patient and not to the organization. They will want – indeed have – an obligation to do the best that they can for their patient. An important organizational consequence of the pursuit of this role is that they use current resources of the organization, and take actions that mortgage future resources.

Doctors will try to get the resources that they think are necessary for their patients, often without considering the wider implications of doing so. Unless they have to ask for more resources, they may not consider the future resource implications of their actions. They may be unwilling to recognize resource constraints.

Chief executives are responsible for maintaining expenditure within budget and ensuring that the service priorities are adhered to. These responsibilities can be threatened by consultants' actions. The role that managers are employed to perform means that they are likely to be viewed with suspicion by doctors, who see them as interfering with their own role of serving the patient. This suspicion is aggravated if the manager seeks to restrict their access to resources or to ensure that doctors' contracts are fulfilled.

Differences in Training and Experience
The relationship between doctors and non-medical managers is made more difficult by differences in their training and careers. Doctors' lengthy and arduous training produces a group with its own culture and

sense of belonging to an elite clan. This is reinforced in those coming from a medical family. *Doctors are trained to think individualistically rather than organizationally;* to have a loyalty to medical ethics but not to the organization that employs them; to pursue their individual goals rather than to consider wider goals, including the needs of their colleagues.

Doctors take the lead in the patient's treatment and grow accustomed to being in command of other services to the patient. They are used to deference from most of those with whom they come in contact: patients, nurses, paramedics and – if they are consultants – from junior doctors. This can breed arrogance and a dismissal of what they may still insist on calling 'administrators', perhaps because they dislike the connotation of 'managers'. At its worst, this arrogance can result in an attitude that is unwilling to consider either the effectiveness of their own performance or its repercussions on others. Because of their powerful position, it is much easier for consultants than for other employees in the NHS to behave with little regard for the difficulties that their attitudes and actions cause for others.

Doctors' work is stressful, as figures for alcoholism and suicides amongst doctors show. Perhaps because of this, they may work on a short fuse and lose their temper more commonly than do other members of staff; they say what they think of others more readily than is usual amongst managers, or even other professional people. The stress under which they work is one of the explanations, as we are all liable to be more irritable when stressed. A further explanation is that because of their powerful position and individualistic role they have had fewer constraints upon their behaviour than is common in organizational life.

Managers learn different skills and attitudes. They *learn to think about their work as part of a larger organization*, which means that they have to cooperate with others, to coordinate their work and that of their department with the work of other departments. They owe a loyalty to the organization and are expected to achieve the objectives set them from above.

Yet *the careers of doctors and managers are likely to produce different attitudes to the hospital*. Consultants are likely to spend 20 or more years in the same hospital, so it will be hard for them not to identify with it. This may not stop them going public when they think patient care is threatened: an action that some trust chairs from industry may find infuriating. Managers, despite owing a loyalty to the organization, will typically move often to forward their careers. They will find it easier to see that closing a hospital may improve patient care.

Managers' success will largely depend upon their ability to influence others, often those over whom they have little or no control and whose work – if they are in charge of people with a different training from their own – they may not fully understand. Doctors can more easily rely upon their professional expertise as the basis for exercising authority; managers must develop interpersonal skills, a capacity to understand the other person's point of view and to think politically about ways of effecting change. They should learn to be diplomatic in their approach to sensitive problems, and skilful in their capacity to motivate the different personalities who work for them. They will often need considerable perseverance and resilience if they are to effect change.

Doctors and managers, therefore, *have different – and potentially conflicting – roles to play.* This makes them look at problems differently. The fact that their training and careers have given them distinctive attitudes, skills and habits of relating to other people makes it even harder for them to understand each other. Managers' training and experience should make it easier for them to bridge the gap of understanding, and to express themselves in language that helps to do so.

Differences in Relative Power

Doctors' powerful position has always posed problems for managers and chairs – and for politicians too – in seeking to make changes that affect doctors. Doctors' fears that management and non-executives with a business approach will affect their power – and, most importantly, their clinical automomy – has increased their suspicions of managerial intentions.

These fears and suspicions have been increased for many doctors by the changes brought in by Conservative governments. An increasing number accept that any government must seek to ensure effective and efficient care, but many fear that patients' needs are not given top priority

Personality Clashes

The intensity of personality clashes that sometimes exists between doctors working in the same hospital is one of the distinctively difficult problems for those responsible for ensuring the provision of good patient care. There are probably two reasons why these personality clashes are a particular problem amongst doctors. One is the fact that doctors tend to stay in the same trust once they become consultants, so that personal feuds can go on for a long time. Another is that doctors have had less need to learn to accommodate to other people.

CHANGES AFFECTING DOCTORS

It is a commonplace to talk about the changes affecting organizations and all those who work in them. Changes often produce defensive reactions. Doctors, particularly hospital doctors, are exposed to an unusually large number of changes and so defensive reactions are to be expected.

There are the changes brought in by Conservative governments from the late 1980s on. But the underlying changes affecting medicine must affect the policies of any government, although the solutions they choose may differ.

A leader in the BMJ, written by Richard Smith, its editor, and Ian Morrison, President of the Institute for the Future, based in California, described the profound structural changes affecting medicine everywhere.[1] They suggested that: 'five key driving forces will continue to transform the practice of medicine well into the next century'. They gave these as:

- the power of big ugly buyers. They argue that power is shifting to purchasers who will increasingly be demanding evidence of effectiveness;
- the rise of sophisticated consumers which will change fundamentally the doctor–patient relationship;
- new technology, arguing that molecular biology and information technology will transform medicine in the next century;
- shifts in the boundaries of health and medicine;
- the ethics of controlling human biology.

It is the first two, and particularly the first, that are likely to cause problems for leaders trying to influence doctors to accept the reality of these changes and not to see them as the evil intent of managers and politicians.

There are also the well-known changes, such as more old people and the availability of costly new treatments that are putting pressure on the costs of health care.

The potential for conflict between doctors and managers – and between doctors themselves in competing for resources – is increased by the financial pressures upon the NHS. The attempts to give greater priority to non-acute services can also cause conflict, since most doctors work in the acute services. Managers have had to take unpopular actions to try to balance the books, and to ensure that resources are distributed in accordance with national priorities for patient care.

Steps towards the ideal

These are about what the individual leader can do, and not about possible institutional changes. Stating the ideal shows what to aim at; you should, as in other chapters, adapt the ideal to your own views and situation. Since attempting to lead doctors is difficult, and can often be discouraging, it is particularly important to have a clear picture of your ideal as stimulus, guide and encouragement. Understanding the nature of the difficulties that can stand in the way of reaching the ideal, and the reasons for them, are also essential steps towards knowing what to do. The first task is:

BRIDGING THE MANAGEMENT/MEDICAL DIVIDE

'Bridging' is the right word, because one would not want there to be no divide, as a report on management development for doctors pointed out:

> a measure of disagreement and conflict between managers and doctors over key issues can actually be good for the Service, in that it subjects such issues to scrutiny from more than one perspective.[2]

It is desirable that problems should be examined both from the managerial perspective of optimizing resources and considering priorities, and from the clinical perspective of doing the best for the individual patient. It is the suspicion of, and misunderstandings about, each other's motives that need to be overcome. *A key task for managers is to show doctors that they are also committed to patient care, but that this commitment necessarily takes a different form.* For doctors, the task is to understand the necessity for, and the nature of, management and what its concepts and tech niques can offer.

Managers, and chairs too, must recognize the very real fears that many doctors have about managerial actions. Their fear is that clinical freedom will be eroded by managers. This is still a powerful factor motivating doctors to resist changes proposed by managers to ensure the most effective use of resources.

There needs to be a growth of mutual understanding which is best fostered by personal contact, within the hospital or practice and at meetings outside. An example of the latter are the meetings for managers and leading medics on new medical developments which managers say they find helpful in understanding medical attitudes, as well as for the specific subjects discussed.

There also needs to be a common understanding of specific issues. Both doctors and managers must realize that it is important to keep each other informed of likely changes and to do so at an early stage so that the possible repercussions can be explored. As one chief executive put it:

> I can't stress too much how important it is to be able to drop in and chat to consultants in a relaxed way. Where I've not done that, thinking perhaps that the issue was sufficiently straightforward or that I didn't have the time, it's nearly always come unstuck or had a rough passage.

ENCOURAGING DOCTORS TO TAKE ON MANAGERIAL ROLES?

This has been government policy since the introduction of general management. There are *strong arguments in favour of doctors' participation in management*. It can bring both a medical perspective to managerial problems and a responsibility for problem resolution. It can help to bridge the medical–management divide. It may be somewhat easier for doctors to manage other doctors, since their credibility for understanding the problems that doctors face should be higher. Above all it has been seen as a good way of getting doctors to accept the need for the efficient use of resources.

Since the late 1980s there has been a major change in the number of doctors participating in management. The appointment of clinical directors and of medical directors on trust boards has been the main route for this. Increasingly doctors have come to accept that some of them should participate in management and have been able to find individuals who were willing to do so. The growth of doctors' participation in management is shown by the establishment of the British Association of Medical Managers and by the conference run in February 1994 by this association together with the BMJ and BMA on 'Every Doctor is a Manager'.

Experience shows that these new leadership roles pose difficulties for the doctors who take them on. There are remediable problems, like doctors' lack of managerial knowledge. Many of the early initiatives sought to tackle this. They have been successful in that doctors taking on managerial roles are now likely to accept that there is a body of knowledge to be learnt and that many will have gone on some kind of management course. They may also have learnt that the authoritarian approach, which is traditional in much medical practice, will often antagonize those with whom they will have to work.

There are other problems, which are intrinsic to employing doctors as part-time managers. There are the tensions that come from trying to combine a part-time managerial job with continuing clinical work. Other problems were shown by a rather discouraging study, by Allan Bruce and Sandra Hill in late 1993, of the Scottish experience. The authors concluded:

Doctors have, for the most part, demonstrated themselves to be fairly reluctant managers. This, coupled with their lack of experience of managerial issues, raises important questions about their future role in management at the expense of clinical activity. It may, therefore, be counterproductive to continue to invest valuable time and effort in encouraging doctors to play a more active role in management when this has resource implications for the NHS. Even though doctors are the most influential group operating within the NHS, it does not mean to

say that the use of their skills, talent and experience in the management of the service represents the most efficient and effective use of
resources.[3]

They also suggest that doctors *'may quite simply be very expensive and
inexperienced managers'.*[4]

A study by Sue Dopson of the reactions of consultants, who had
attended specially designed management programmes at Templeton
College, Oxford, found similar concerns. She found these doctors asking
themselves troubled questions, for example:

> Is my involvement in management actually benefiting patients? Is
> taking on a management role worth the aggravation with colleagues
> and worth the increased time and effort put into my work life at the
> expense of home life? Time devoted to management is time away from
> patients and research that might benefit patient care, is this ethical?
> Why spend thousands of pounds on my management development
> needs when there are managers in the NHS whom I could advise?[5]

*We need doctors who will lead their fellows to accept the challenges facing
medicine today and the importance of making the most efficient use of resources.
What is less clear, from the evidence so far, is whether doctors in part-time management roles is the best way to develop, and to use, such leadership abilities.*
Doctors do need a better understanding of the nature of, and necessity
for, management. But working in a managerial role is not the only way
of getting this.

In general practice, the trend is the other way: to employ managers to
relieve the GP from administrative and managerial tasks. This ranges
from the growth of a new occupational role, that of practice manager, to
the advertisement by the Potteries GP Fundholding Consortium, covering 28 general practices, for a chief executive, which asked for: 'solid
general management capability', 'impeccable interpersonal skills', an
'accomplished change manager', and one who will 'fully appreciate the
strategic agenda'.[6] These new management posts also provide new areas
for managerial leadership.

So far the discussion has emphasized the value of doctors taking part
in management, while recognizing some of the problems of this.
However, a different perspective questions whether it is desirable to
have doctors exercising yet more influence by taking on a managerial
role. David Hunter, for example, has emphasized the bias towards acute
medicine at the expense of a broader view of what makes for a healthy
life. He has suggested:

> Doctors as managers may make it that much more difficult for non-
> medical managers and policy makers to pursue an alternative vision of

what a health policy, and health improvement system, might look like.[7]

DEVELOPING INFORMATION SYSTEMS FOR DOCTORS TO USE

This is happening, but more slowly in hospitals than in general practice. Industry is still far ahead of medical practice in using information technology as an aid to decision-taking.

USING THE GENERAL METHODS OF CHANGE MANAGEMENT

These methods, which were briefly discussed on p. 19, are relevant to any leader who is seeking to effect change. They are particularly important for leaders in their relations with doctors because of the difficulties posed by the unusual combination of strong individualism with clannish support if one of their number is seen to be threatened by an outsider – that is, someone who does not belong to the medical clan. Even medical or clinical directors may be seen as having 'changed sides'.

Where the proposed change is likely to be unpopular with doctors, remember that *the first stage of the change process is 'unfreezing' attitudes*. Be on the lookout for events that may encourage unfreezing, when doctors may be more understanding of the need for change, and hence more willing to accept it. Such opportunities may come, for example, from an unfavourable report on an aspect of the hospital's medical care, or from a major financial crisis.

Develop your strategy for achieving change; agree what you are aiming at with those whose support you need, then plan how you can overcome doctors' potentially powerful antagonism to change. There are three steps:

1. *Discover Who Matters*
   (a) Who are the opinion leaders?
   (b) Who are potential allies, and who will at least be neutral?
   (c) Who are, or could be, dangerous opponents?
   (d) Who are good sources of information about medical reactions?
   (e) Who would be good at contributing to management?

2. *Understand Leading Individuals*
   Study the leading doctors: what matters most to them; what are their concerns; what upsets them; and what skills could they contribute to resolving a problem or pushing forward a change?

3. *Enlist Support*
   (a) Show understanding of the situation that doctors (especially leading doctors) are dealing with – this may require prior work on

your part – and seek to build goodwill by trying to help with their problems.

(b) Gain doctors' respect by providing an efficient service for them

(c) Get doctors' interested in solving a problem by asking for their help or giving the problem to them to solve – an old ploy, but one that can work particularly well with doctors because they are intelligent, are used to and enjoy problem solving and may like to demonstrate their superior ability.

(d) Use the right language in talking with doctors: talk about 'improving the organization of patient care', rather than using management words like 'efficiency' that can grate on medical ears.

(e) Finally, show you are trustworthy. This may seem to go against the machiavellian advice that is implicit in some of the points above, especially 'discover who matters', but political calculation is not incompatible with trustworthiness in the sense of keeping to one's word. That is vital because trust once lost is hard, often impossible, to regain, as John Harvey-Jones points out:

> Trust, once it begins to deteriorate, quite suddenly flips over and becomes a sort of galloping corrosion of suspicion which is very difficult to halt. Trust is tremendously difficult to build up and all too easy to destroy, so it is worth taking all sorts of actions, even if they appear to be finicky, to avoid losing it.[8]

This is useful advice in all relationships, but it is of the utmost importance to the relationship between managers and doctors because the danger of doctors being suspicious of managers' actions, even if they are doctors themselves, is greater than in most, perhaps all other, relationships.

Leading doctors to understand managerial problems and to be willing to help to solve them is one of the most difficult leadership tasks for chairs, chief executives and public health directors. It requires vision, courage, persistence, understanding and skill. It is to be hoped that more doctors who have the skill, or the ability to acquire it, will take up this challenging leadership task and seek to achieve the ideals suggested earlier.

Summary

1. If you are in a position to influence doctors, you have a key leadership task. The *ideals to be pursued are that the doctors will*:

(a) understand the need for, and be willing to contribute to and to learn about, management;

(b) recognize other views of health policy and health improvement;
(c) place concern for patient care above professional loyalty;
(d) recognize that others' need for more resources may be greater than theirs;
(e) be active in reviewing their own performance;
(f) treat other contributors to patient care as team members;
(g) recognize and adjust to the changing roles of other professions;
(j) treat patients as intelligent individuals.

2. The *main ideals for managers in seeking to lead doctors* is that they will:

(a) be resiliently proactive in trying to achieve the ideals listed above;
(b) be seen as the trusted arbitrator between different medical interests;
(c) express the corporate values and goals in a way that makes sense to doctors;
(d) provide an efficient and sympathetic service to doctors, so that they can give of their best;

An ideal that should be common to both doctors and managers who are not doctors is that they will recognize and seek to understand each other's different viewpoints.
3. The main ideal for trust chairs is to realize the importance of understanding doctors' points of view and of enlisting their cooperation:

The *major difficulties in reaching the ideal* stem from differences in the role of doctors and managers, so that they see problems differently. For managers who are not doctors, this is accentuated by differences in their training and experience. Doctors' powerful positions make it hard to get changes accepted that they do not see as beneficial.

The main *steps* that you should take *towards achieving the ideal*, whatever your professional background are:

(a) seek to foster mutual understanding;
(b) encourage doctors to contribute to management; or if you are a doctor, consider doing so; but be aware of the problems of a part-time managerial role;
(c) provide management training for doctors; and if you are a doctor, accept the need for such training;
(d) develop information systems that are useful to doctors;
(e) recognize the difficulties of implementing change and apply the guidelines for managing change:

● identify whose opinions are most important to achieving a particular change;

● seek to understand their motivation;
● present the change in language that is acceptable to doctors;
● enlist support.

(f)   Above all, show that you are trustworthy.

CHAPTER 5

Sharing the leadership: chair and chief executive

'It is remarkable how well you and the chief executive gell, so that you each come in as appropriate.'
(An observer of a meeting commenting to the chair)

A special aspect of being a leader at the top of some organizations is that the leadership *has to be shared*. The most common form of sharing at the top is, as in the NHS, between the chair and the chief executive. It is this relationship that will be analysed here in the same format as before: ideal, difficulties in the way of achieving the ideal and steps forward. In the next chapter we shall look at the sharing that takes place in teams at different levels in the organization.

The ideal

1. **The sharing of work is complementary, so that the two together achieve more than they could do independently**. They should make the best use of each other's *different roles*, and of their *relative strengths*.

   There are core aspects of the leadership role in the chair's and in the chief executive's jobs. The *chair is the figurehead* for the district, and should play that aspect of the leadership role on public occasions, particularly where the policies of the authority or board are under attack. The *chair is also the leader of the board*. The *chief executive should lead the staff*, and particularly the senior managers, and the chair should do nothing to undermine that leadership by being seen as a way of bypassing the chief executive. These are the roles that each should play, that is the 'demand' part of the leadership in each job. The leadership role is necessarily shared between the chair and the chief executive, though the extent to which it is shared, and how it is shared, will vary depending upon the situation, the personalities and their choices. (See pp. 184–6 for an explanation of demands and choices and how they can help in understanding the role sharing between chairs and chief executives.[1])

Chairs have the problem of learning to understand both their own role, and the strengths and weaknesses of the chief executive. They may need to learn what role they want to play, and how this best fits with that played by the chief executive. They may think that their chief executive should be playing a stronger leadership role, and be concerned about how to get him or her to do so.

2. **It is a partnership: the two work in tandem on major changes and negotiations**.
3. **The chair needs to retain a visible independence of the managers,** so as not to be seen as the managers' mouthpiece. Also as the chief executive's boss the chair must assess his or her performance, difficult though it may sometimes be for a chair without experience of the NHS to do so effectively.
4. **The chair gives more than the minimum time that is required to perform the demand aspects of the role.** The time that the chair gives to the job obviously affects the opportunities for sharing work, that is not exclusively the chief executive's, according to knowledge, experience and personality.
5. **The chief executive should be able to use their chair as a person that they can turn to for advice, help and support** in what is often a lonely job, particularly in times of difficulty.
6. **The chair should be concerned about, and seek to assist the development of, their chief executive**.

Difficulties in the way of effective sharing

The difficulties for both chair and chief executive come from accommodating their own leadership role to that played by the other. The difficulties are usually greater for the chief executive because chairs are in a stronger position to determine how they want to play their role. The difficulties that can arise were described, as follows, by the district general managers who were part of the Templeton tracer study of DGMs.[2] They remain as true today:

1. **The time that the chair gives to the job**. This may be too little – a day a week or less – to act as a leader except in meetings of the board. The chief executive may then feel that the chair's leadership and support is not available when required, particularly on difficult public occasions. Alternatively, the chair may work almost or wholly full-time; then the chief executive's difficulty is likely to be that the chair wants to do *too much*, thus infringing on the chief executive's own role.

2. **The chair's inadequate knowledge of the NHS**. A chair with no previous knowledge can take a lot of the chief executive's time during the induction period. The chief executive may also be anxious about an inexperienced chair saying the wrong thing in public or in difficult negotiations.
3. **The chair's view of the role may differ from that which the chief executive thinks is correct**. Taking the lead where the chief executive thinks it inappropriate, for example, or failing to do so when the chief executive thinks the chair should.
4. **Chief executives will commonly be concerned if they think that the chair is undermining their position in some way**. This can be either by supporting members of their own staff against them, or by taking a different stance in board meetings from that indicated in prior discussions.
5. **A chair who is unable or unwilling to lead the board discussions**. Such a chair will also cause the chief executive difficulty. If the chair lacks the skills to guide the discussion, that is a legitimate source of concern for the chief executive. However,the chair may be unwilling to do so, believing that the aim should be to ensure that the subjects are well discussed and not to steer the discussion towards the conclusions desired by the managers, even if they were agreed at a briefing meeting. Non-executive members are likely to think that such neutral chairing is the appropriate use of the chair's role!
6. **Chairs may have a problem of reconciling the role that the regional policy board member wants them to play with the expectations of their own board members and of the chief executive**.

These difficulties are all expressed from the point of view of the chief executive but chairs may have their own problems as well.

7. **The chair is inadequately briefed about current or potential problems**.
8. **The chair is concerned about how the chief executive does the job and has been unable to get him or her to change sufficiently yet is reluctant to get rid of the chief executive because of the resulting upheaval**.

Steps towards the ideal

The relationship between the chair and the chief executive resembles that of a marriage. It has some of the same difficulties, and needs some of the same insights and tact. Both partners have to *learn to work together* and to evolve the *particular roles* that each plays. In a marriage, the division of roles and of tasks is more fluid because nowadays there is no clear guide as to who does what in the house or outside it. The roles of chair and of chief executive are more defined, but even so there can be great variation in practice as the Templeton tracer study of 20 DGMs showed.[3]

Both need to learn to understand each other's *strengths and weaknesses*, and to establish a sufficiently close relationship that they can discuss how they can make best use of their partnership. They should agree on their strategy in negotiations and in handling problems that have aroused – or are likely to arouse – public controversy. They also need to agree on the role that they are each going to play in negotiations and public meetings.

There are also specific steps that each should take to achieve the ideal, which are now listed separately.

CHAIRS

Chairs should ask themselves: 'what can I most usefully contribute in my organization, apart from the work that I must do?'

1. **The prime role is to lead the authority or trust board**. Doing that effectively requires a good understanding of the issues to be discussed, an understanding of the different viewpoints amongst the members, and of their likely reactions. This means ensuring that the managers provide good briefing and having other sources of information as well.
2. **There is an important role in providing a more detached view of problems, and often a wider experience than the chief executive and other senior managers can have**. The chair should ensure that the chief executive and senior managers think through the philosophy underlying the policies.
3. **The chair plays a leadership role on public occasions**, particularly when the authority or trust is under attack.
4. **The chair may need to encourage the chief executive to act more like a leader**. How necessary this is will depend upon the chief executive's personality and background. **A few chairs may need to do the opposite, to restrain the chief executive from taking too forceful a lead** when that may be bad tactics, or to give senior managers more headroom.
5. **The chair has potentially a very important role in stimulating the chief executive to learn to be a more effective manager**. It is all too easy for senior managers to think that by the time they have reached a top job they have nothing more they need to learn about managing. This may be less of a danger today with younger appointments.
6. **In hospitals, the leading consultants will want to have discussions with the chair and to be sure that their views are known and sym-**

pathetically understood. If the consultants are not satisfied they may, as examples have shown, take a vote of no confidence in the chair.

7. **Recognition of the good work done by other staff – especially by nurses,** as the most numerous staff in most trusts and those who are in particularly stressful jobs. This is an important potential part of the chair's role as figurehead. Attending staff occasions like prize giving can help to show recognition of good work.

8. **In commissioning organizations there may be times when problems with a provider that have not been resolved by the chief executives should be discussed by the respective chairs.**

There are many other ways in which the chair could usefully take a lead, particularly if the chief executive is not doing so. The chair may, for example, need to ensure that the chief executive and other senior managers adequately *clarify their objectives,* though that ought to be the chief executive's task. There may be a need, too, to ensure that more is done to get *community views and real feedback* about patients' views.

To give a different kind of example, a chair with good external contacts can be a source of information about what is happening in the local community and outside it and seek, if necessary, to *broaden the knowledge and interests* of the chief executive and other senior managers. A skilful, politically knowledgeable chair can also take the lead in relations with MPs and in some negotiations. **The division of leadership should depend very much upon the relative skills, knowledge and interests of the chair and the chief executive.**

CHIEF EXECUTIVE

Part of the skill of being a chief executive is establishing a productive relationship with the chair, making the best use of the time and abilities that he or she can contribute. It should be possible to do so with most chairs, even if difficult and egocentric, provided you are able to look at them unemotionally and recognize what are the best ways to influence them. The Templeton study of district general managers showed that this can be very difficult for chief executives to do. It is all too easy for them to feel so emotionally about what they see to be the chair's failings that they cannot take a strategic view of how to make best use of their chair.

1. **Consider what the chair wants from the job, and try to provide it:** some, for example, may enjoy public recognition by taking part in public occasions.

2. **Do not underrate what the chair can contribute,** as a number of the district general managers in the Templeton study did. Learn to understand the strengths and weaknesses of the chair in comparison

with your own and **try to use the chair to achieve the first ideal given at the start of the chapter**. Take a positive view of what the chair can contribute rather than overrating the importance of what you do, or deploring what you do not like about your chair.

3. Use your chair, if possible, **as one way of learning about what is happening in the community**, or outside it.
4. **Seek to enhance the chair's credibility in the oganization**: for example, try to present the chair's demands on other staff in a positive light, such as saying that they come from an interest in patient care.
5. **Make the best use of your time with chairs who have little time to spend** by arranging meetings well in advance, and making sure that briefings are succinct and informative.
6. Make sure that the chair is **adequately briefed about problems** and for any public meeting.
7. Recognize the value that staff in general, and in hospital trusts that consultants in particular, can place on having contact with the chair and, if necessary **help the chair to understand how to relate to consultants without undermining management**.

Summary

1. A few jobs *require leadership to be shared*. In the NHS this is true for the relationship between the chair and the chief executive.
2. The ideal relationship between chair and chief executive is a *complementary one* that enables them jointly to contribute more to the organization than they could do independently. The ideal is a partnership that makes the best use of the differences in their roles and in their abilities and experience.
3. In achieving the ideal, there need to be some of the same insights and tact that characterize successful marriages. Both partners need to learn to understand each other's strengths and weaknesses.
4. Chairs should develop the chief executive's leadership abilities, particularly if he or she is inexperienced. They should also use their status where it will help in negotiations and to show appreciation of good work. They should be careful not to usurp part of the chief executive's role.
5. One of the skills of being an effective chief executive is establishing a productive relationship with the chair. Good use should be made of his or her experience and abilities and clear briefing provided on issues.
6. Realize that sharing leadership effectively extends what you can achieve as a leader.

CHAPTER 6

Sharing the leadership: team-working

'A shift towards more team working within the Department could bring great benefits in terms of flexibility, efficiency and effectiveness, and improved job satisfaction. This would involve greater emphasis on the work to be done, and less on the formal building blocks of organizational structure. Teams should contain within them all the necessary skills and authority to perform a task, and should take responsibility for doing it properly without the need for external approvals and quality checks. Putting new ways of working into practice will take years rather than months.'

(Review of the Wider Department of Health)[1]

Being a manager is much more difficult than it used to be because of the many changes taking place. It also requires a *different form of working to cope with rapid change. Teamworking now often takes the place of the traditional hierarchy* because experience, embodied in rules and in the knowledge of the boss, is no longer an adequate guide to what should be done. In times of uncertainty, all may have useful ideas and information about the best way forward. An even more important reason for teamworking is that changes are only implemented successfully if people are actively involved.

For the leader there are many advantages in the new style of working. People are more committed to their work than they used to be in the past, hence there is less need for supervision. However, traditional style leaders have to learn new skills. Temperamentally some leaders are comfortable working through a team, but others find it hard to adapt a naturally directive approach to the more consensual style needed in a team. *They have to learn the value of sharing the leadership.*

Such sharing, research has shown, naturally takes place in groups. Next time you are in a working group watch what happens. You will notice that *different people take the lead at different times because they make a distinctive contribution.* The leadership roles most easily observed are: focusing members on the task to be done; summing up; seeking to smooth any personality clashes and contributing a new idea that changes the subject of the discussion. You may notice the same people playing a similar role in another group.

Teams do not have bosses. They have leaders, more than one because of the different kinds of leadership required. In top management teams the chief executive will be the formal leader, but if it is really a team others will at times take the lead to move the group forward.

TEAMWORKING

The word 'team' is fashionable and hence used too widely to describe groups that are not really teams. Sometimes, as in 'primary care team', the phrase is used to highlight a change that has been taking place towards involving a variety of people in decision-making.

Since NHS managers spend so much of their time in meetings, it is worthwhile asking oneself which of these meetings ought to be, but are not, teams? It is useful to ask too whether the team members could work together more effectively. A useful definition of teamwork is:

> Work done by a number of associated people who are all agreed on and committed to doing it. Each person does a part of the work and his part is coordinated with the efforts of others.

> (French and Saward, *The Dictionary of Management*)[2]

The great strength of teamworking is that the members are committed because they identify with a common goal. In an effective team there is a synergy amongst the different individual contributions and all need to contribute for the team to be successful.

In some activities teamworking is essential for success: football and surgery are two of the better known examples, because:

> Once teams get into the swing of working well together, they are one of the few ways of consistently managing complex and competing elements over a long period of time.[3]

There is a warning note in the quotation above: 'once they get into the swing of working well together'. It takes time for that to happen and teams differ in the quality of their performance, as we know from football. Nor does it happen automatically with time.

This chapter is about how to create an effective team and about the leadership implications of teamworking. It uses the same format as for the other chapters: the ideal, difficulties and steps forward.

DIFFERENT TYPES OF TEAMS

There are many different kinds of teams:

1. Most common are problem-solving teams composed of the immediate work group, which will usually also do some work planning.
2. Project teams which are set up for a particular purpose and are short-lived.
3. Linking teams, which are inter-departmental or inter-agency. These may be the hardest groups to develop as teams.

The general discussion of ideal, difficulties and steps forward applies to them all, but the leadership will vary. In some, such as a clinical psychiatric team, the consultant will be the leader, but what does this mean? Andrew Sims, President of the Royal College of Psychiatry writing with an academic, David Sims, say:

> Different types of leaders are required for different activities. The consultant should be considered the titular leader, for example for the referral of new patients by the GP, and the consultant has a role in developing leadership potential in other members of the team.
> But perhaps the essential role is that of problem construction; identifying the exact problem that needs to be addressed for each individual patient on each occasion...
> Leadership should not be seen as the consultant's prerogative. Leadership dispersal aims to develop the individual skills and potential of each member of the team.[4]

The ideal

It is that all team members will:

1. **Agree on the goal of their activities.**
2. **Feel a commitment to it and strive to achieve it.**

   These two are common to all kinds of teams, but otherwise there are different ideals for teams that are engaged in a common physical activity from those whose activities are intellectual. An ideal for the former type of team is that:

3. **Members will follow the leader when necessary.** In such teams effectiveness will always require a formal leader to ensure coordination.

Most teams in the NHS will be of the other kind **where the task is an intellectual one**. For such teams further ideals are that **members:**

4. **Are willing to express divergent views.**
5. **Are willing to listen and seek to make use of divergent views.**
6. **Will critically consider different possible solutions** to problems posed.
7. **Will make their own distinctive contribution to the group and encourage others to do so too.** The latter, especially, is the task of the team leader.
8. **Decisions are usually based on consensus,** not majority vote or the formal leader's diktat.

Difficulties in the way

The ideals for effective team working show that it is not easy to achieve. The most common difficulties are:

1. **The team allows some issue to become more important than its own performance.** This may be personal antagonisms and/or conflicts of interest within the group which are allowed to interfere with the effective working of the team. It may be complaints about others so that too much time is spent on 'us and them' concerns. Or it may be pursuing personal agendas. Keeping the group focused on the task requires skilled leadership including a sensitivity to the dynamics of the group.
2. Conversely, **the group may too easily reach agreement** without critically examining the real problems and appraising different alternative solutions.
   There is a delicate balance to be struck between encouraging cooperation without discouraging the expression of different views.
3. One of the difficulties for the team leader may be **learning to be comfortable working as a team leader rather than the traditional boss.** This **can be especially difficult for doctors** who have traditionally been treated with deference by other professions.

The difficulties above are about the working of the group; there may also be problems in its composition.

4. **The group may be badly balanced** – much of Meredith Belbin's work on effective teams[5] has been about the mix of skills required. But in organizations there may be little or no choice in the composition of the team, particularly when it is a cross-agency one.
   Where a group is badly balanced, the job of the team leader becomes particularly important in seeking to restrain the vociferous and domineering, and in encouraging the quieter members. The team leader

may also recognize a need to bring in missing skills from outside the group.

5. The team may contain a weak member and **the team leader may be unwilling to confront and to resolve problems of poor individual performance.**

6. **There is a lack of recognition for team as distinct from individual achievement.** This can be a difficulty where personal rewards or promotion prospects are linked to individual achievement and do not take account of team contributions.

Steps towards the ideal

There is widespread recognition in the NHS of the need for teambuilding; hence the popularity of away days. So the first two steps will be familiar.

1. **Recognize that a team spirit needs to be developed.**

2. **Take time** – and away days are a means of ensuring the necessary time is taken – **to enable team members to work together in agreeing goals and identifying problems.**

3. **Be aware of the common difficulties in teamworking** mentioned above and be alert to their presence in the group.

4. **A skilled team facilitator** can help on occasions, but may not be needed and may not be sufficiently skilled.

5. **A perceptive leader will learn what roles they are good at playing themselves and look for others to complement them.** If you are very task oriented it is useful, indeed it may be essential, to have someone who is more sensitive to what is happening within the group and good at defusing potential personality clashes.

6. **Realize when a member of your staff is in a position to be more effective than you are.** For example, there are choices to be made in the relative roles to be played by the chief executive and the medical director in a hospital trust.

4. Recognize that **asking the right questions is the most important first task** in planning, and one that is usually more difficult than it seems initially. It is a task that a good team will do better than an individual.

7. **Beware thinking that a report is the output of team endeavour.** It may sometimes be the purpose of a particular group, but for executive groups successful implementation is essential. A lot of time is often spent in the NHS producing reports which are never implemented.

8. **If you are putting together a project team think about the contributions that people make not just in terms of their knowledge and experience but also of their personality and hence the role that they are likely to play in the team.**

Belbin's book on *Management Teams*[6] is a useful guide to the different roles that need to be played, and to what happens if you get the mix wrong. Even when you cannot choose the members of a working group, a knowledge of team roles can still be useful. Belbin's analysis shows that individuals may prefer to play one role but can often play another. If you notice that the group tends to be weak in particular ways – such as failing to reach decisions or being very limited in its ideas – then ask yourself whether you can supply the missing ingredient ('particular team role' in Belbin's language), or whether there is another member of the group who has the ability, and whom you can encourage to do so.

One of the encouraging aspects of being the leader of a team is that the work is a mutual endeavour. Once a team is working together effectively, less is required of the leader than of a traditional boss. But getting to that stage is, as we have seen, difficult. *Team working can be much more effective than hierarchical working, but it is more difficult to do well.* Learning to do so takes skill, knowledge of effective team working and time to develop the trust required and the understanding of what each member can contribute. Recognizing the difficulties is the first step.

You may want to ask yourself whether your immediate group of staff or, say, the cross-agency group of which you are a member, is working well as a team. The following are some guides:

- there is a lot of energy when the group meets;
- members are supportive of each other;
- there is trust and respect;
- there is candid feedback;
- members enjoy meeting together but without developing an 'us and them' feeling;
- members agree on, and are committed to, the group's goals.

These guides are all about the conditions for achievement: conditions that distinguish a team from hierarchical working. How much the team actually achieves will depend upon the quality of management; the calibre of the people; and their ability to do well, management tasks like setting goals, developing strategy and developing a plan which follows through to implementation.

Summary

Teamworking is now often used instead of hierarchical working because it is more suited to rapid change. People who work in teams are more committed to their work. This means less supervision is necessary, but traditional style managers will have to learn to share their leadership. They will have to learn to understand group working and to become skilful in teambuilding.

The *ideals* for teamworking include:
- agreement on, and commitment to, the team's objectives;
- making good use of the distinctive contribution of individuals;
- most decisions are reached by consensus.

The main *difficulties* are:
- allowing some issue to distract from performance;
- too much consensus so agreement is reached too easily;
- a badly balanced group.

The key *steps towards the ideal* are:
- take time to team build;
- be alert to the common difficulties in teamworking.

The overall lesson for any manager, but particularly a senior one, of this chapter and the previous is that there are different aspects to leadership and that these often will – and should be – shared. This is reassuring because it means that you do not have to be good at everything; indeed you will not have the ability – or the time – to be that. What you do need is an ability to recognize your own strengths and weaknesses and those of the people with whom you work, and the leadership ability to get them to complement you.

CHAPTER 7

Leadership and the board

'As an employee I should be assessed, even if the trust is performing well it depends upon how high are the standards of performance. The year on year contribution of the chair and non-executives ought to be assessed. No-one is looking at the role of non-executives and they should be.'

(trust chair)

The chair is the official leader of the board, but this leadership may, and usually will, be shared with the chief executive as discussed in Chapter 5. Chairs are constrained in their leadership of the board by: the time that they give to the job, their understanding of the issues, the attitudes of the members to their leadership, and the role played by the chief executive. All of these they can seek to change, but it remains a difficult role to play.

The chief executive mainly exercises leadership in the board by influencing the chair, although personal contact with members provides another opportunity to do so. The chief executive is also influencing the role that non-executives can play, by the issues that are presented and in how they are presented to the board. The management of information is one of the tools in the chief executive's kitbag.

This chapter is based on two related assumptions:

- the main rationale for an NHS board is to provide for public accountability, within national priorities, on the nature of the health care provided;
- the chair, managers and members should share certain ideals if the board is to be effective.

The reorganizations introduced by the Conservatives with *Working for Patients* from 1989[1], produced two major changes which affected some of the issues that arise in leadership on boards. One, was reducing the size of district health authorities and changing their composition. Local authority nominees were abolished and executive members in addition to the chief executive were introduced. As Lynn Ashburner and Liz Cairncross said, reporting on their study of NHS authorities and trust boards:

Overall, the move is away from the representation of a wide range of interests. The emphasis is now placed more on the professional inputs of the NHS manager, and the imported skills and experience of the non-executive expert.[2]

(Though the use of the word 'expert' seems inappropriate for the wide variety of people serving on boards!) Professional representation remained on the Family Health Services Authority while it continued to exist. The other major change was the introduction of trust boards modelled, like the health authority, on company boards with executive and non-executive members.

A change of government might lead to a change in the composition of boards to introduce more local accountability, but many of the problems of board leadership will remain the same. However, the changes in board composition introduced by *Working for Patients*, as Ferlie, Ashburner and Fitzgerald point out, do change the ways in which authority meetings are conducted:

...overt party political disagreements were found to be very rare at Authority meetings. This is a major change from the pre-1990 situation, at least in the urban areas. Instead a consensus emerged after discussion and votes were almost unknown. There was a strong norm of politeness. This is not to say that the non-executives were passive, indeed they could be seen as generally more active than the old DHA members.[3]

One reason for the greater politeness of boards now may be that the new members are more emotionally detached from the issues that they are discussing. They are a privileged group who may well make little use of the NHS.

A comparison of the behaviour of the board of three DHAs and four acute NHS trusts suggests that the role of non-executives in the two may differ. In the districts the

non-executives probed and sought further information, but seldom shaped strategic decisions and only rarely confronted the executive... There were signs of a progression towards a more strategic role over time, but this could collapse if experienced non-executives were pulled out to head up NHS trusts.[4]

On the NHS trusts, it was notable that the executives were comparatively new to their corporate roles and appeared more willing to open up a debate with non-executives, even to the point of actively seeking advice.

Overall, the authors suggest that the new boards are a 'significant break with the "rubber stamping" model of the past';[5] though an earlier study suggested that 'rubber stamp' gives a misleading picture, as implying that they had no influence:

> ...our findings suggest that the DHA, informally or even just by its very existence, exerts considerable influence.[6]

The ideal

The major overall ideal is that the chair, chief executive, executives and non-executives should share common values, trust each other, and jointly seek to use the board to contribute to the provision of the best possible care, taking account of local interests and needs, within national policies and the resources available. The focus of this chapter is on what can be done by individual leaders, whether the chair, chief executive or other board members, to further the ideal.

Ideally the board should play the following roles:

1. **Act as the voice of the community in discussing managerial policies and actions.** What Kenneth Clarke said in an address to NAHA's 1986 annual general meeting remains true despite the subsequent re-organizations and the change from 'members' to 'directors':

> There are three areas in which members need to respond to the voice of the community they serve – informing themselves about public expectations, informing the public about the service locally and finally accounting to the public for the service provided.[7]

2. **Define and monitor the standard of care provided.**
3. **Seek to ensure that cost-effective care is provided.**
4. **Promote the practice of evidence based medicine.**
5. **Seek to enhance staff morale by showing appreciation of good performance.**

The above apply to boards of both health authorities and trusts. There is a further ideal for the former:

6. **Judge the relative priority of the demands made by the different interest groups in the community within the framework of national policies.**

The ideals for working together are that:

1. **All observe the highest standards of individual and corporate probity.**
2. **The non-executives distance themselves from the executive members so that they are able to contribute an outside perspective and to ensure that patient needs are never forgotten.**
3. **The chief executive and other execvtive members accept that the board has a useful role to play and do their best to help the chair and non-executives to play that role.** They recognize the value of having their priorities for care and the assumptions underlying their recommendations challenged, particularly if it is done constructively, and realize that there is always a danger of public servants thinking that they know best what is good for the public.
4. **The abilities of individual non-executives are used,** and they feel that they are making a useful contribution to the provision of good and efficient health care.
5. **Non-executives' time is used efficiently and they get the information that they need.**
6. **All accept that the organization is part of a national health service with the constraints that that imposes, and the need to take hard decisions about priorities.**

Difficulties in achieving the ideal

1. **Ambiguities in the board's role** still exist, especially in the health authority, as the Templeton issue study on the DHA put it:

   > Are they there to check the details, shape the principles, or both? To make active policy decisions or simply to vet the decisions of managers? To ensure that NHS policy is carried out within the constraints of local conditions, or to ensure that local needs are met within the constraints of government policy? To be lay managers themselves, or a public watchdog on professional managers? To provide a public forum of accountability, or to be the public voice in meetings behind the scenes? We have found members and managers with strong views for and against all these positions.[8]

   Even if all involved are clear about the role of the board, there is still the problem of achieving a good balance between adhering to national priorities and satisfying local needs.
2. **The belief amongst some managers that the board is, and should be, mainly a rubber stamp.**
3. **Getting sufficient able non-executive directors who come from various backgrounds and who can give enough time to the work.**

4. **Turnover in membership** which makes consistency of policies and the development of members' knowledge and contribution more difficult.
5. **Non-executives' problems in digesting the information provided and understanding the complexity of some of the issues, particularly in limited time.**
6. **The danger that non-executives will underestimate the effort required to prepare themselves for their responsibilities,** both in understanding current health issues and in acquiring detailed local knowledge of the services for which they are responsible.
7. **The danger of being too cohesive so that there is little real challenge.** Ferlie, Ashburner and Fitzgerald, in their study of NHS boards 1990–92, speculate that this:

> could carry the danger of a Board developing a 'bunker mentality', screening out negative feedback from doctors, staff and the public and badly underestimating the unpopularity of its own actions. Nor may it be able to manage effectively a transition from the current policy paradigm to a future one, should this prove necessary.[9]

8. **Problems arising from the mismatch that can exist between what is good for patients and what is good for staff.** Charlotte Williamson pointed this out in 1986 but it remains true today:

> Changes made towards better non-clinical care for patients are often made at a cost to staff. More choice and control for patients can mean less choice and control for staff. More autonomy for patients can mean less emotional dependency on staff, as well as less compliant behaviour towards them.[10]

She defined non-clinical care as that affecting patients' psychological or social welfare.

Steps towards the ideal

This array of difficulties may make the ideal seem too difficult to attain, yet the process of getting there is well known. Many of the methods have already been discussed in the chapter on leadership in teams. Some boards come nearer to the ideals than others. Some, of course, have abler and better matched and contrasted members and an able chair, but all can probably improve by the following steps, if they have not already been taken:

1. **Agree the values that the board should operate by, that is how they wish to behave to the patients, public, staff and each other.**
2. **Provide the necessary induction for new members**, both for executive members on their corporate role, and for non-executives especially if they are not familiar with the NHS or with the particular organization.
3. **Review the working of the board**. A method that has been used with some success in a number of boards is to establish a joint working group, perhaps with a facilitator, to examine the working of the board and to consider how it can work more effectively. Suggestions for improvement that come from such reviews are:

(a) **Clarify what the board should be discussing**. This needs to be done concretely rather than in abstract terms, like 'policy' – a word which is overworked in the NHS! Lynn Ashburner and Ewan Ferlie reporting on their study of NHS boards said that few boards had explicitly sought to decide what should go to the board and whether they went for information, discussion, decision or for review. It was the chief executive, often in discussion with other executive staff, who decided. The researchers stress the importance of the board defining their strategic role and distinguishing it from the executive role.[11]
(b) **Clarify the role that non-executives can most usefully perform and help them to play it**. Charlotte Williamson pointed out in 1994 that non-executive directors are increasingly frustrated by the difficulties of understanding their organization and its problems and by feeling that the crucial decisions are taken by the chair and the chief executive.[12]
Non-executives can set their own objectives for what they want to contribute in the next year.
(c) **Plan the agenda ahead** to include regular reviews of performance, agreed subjects to be considered at particular meetings together with space for discussing unexpected subjects of concern. Select a very few subjects that merit special attention in the next year. **Ensure that there are opportunities for discussion on selected key problems before papers are presented to a formal meeting of the board**. Reserving some of the meetings for seminars is one way to do this.
(d) **Agree what information is required by the board and make it as digestible and informative as possible**. Specifically, review what performance standards have been set and what monitoring information is provided to check on their achievement. In trusts, non-executives should satisfy themselves that the standards of non-clinical care, as defined above by Charlotte Williamson, are high. This should be one of the purposes of visits.

(e) **Chairs need to be good at chairing board meetings**. Chairs without experience should recognize that they may benefit from training and from observing how other chairs, who have a good reputation for their skill in doing so, handle the meeting.

4. **Non-executives should cultivate as wide a variety of local contacts as they can** with managers and other staff, region, local authorities, GPs, non-executives on other boards and voluntary bodies. Doing so will improve their understanding of what is happening that affects the health service in their area and can provide managers with more information.

Many of the difficulties listed above suggest that **the most important steps are those that can improve mutual trust, clarify the role that members can most usefully perform and help them to play it**. These are useful steps towards achieving the ideal, but it is the spirit in which they are undertaken by chairs, executives and non-executives that is most important. All need to want to make them work but to do so they must also be realistic about the constraints of time and knowledge that limit what non-executives can do. It is in their appointment and monitoring roles that they can make their greatest contribution.

Many of the opportunities for taking a lead in the board necessarily take place at meetings, hence the discussion of sharing leadership within a team, in Chapter 6, is relevant for all those involved.

Summary

THE IDEAL

The major ideal is to develop shared values and trust between chair, chief executive and other members of the board. All those involved should seek to ensure that the board plays the following roles:

● responds to the community it serves;
● judges the relative priority of different interests within national policies;
● defines and monitors the standard of care;
● promotes evidence based medicine;
● reviews the cost-effectiveness of services;
● shows appreciation of good staff performance.

The chief executive and other executives should accept that the board has a useful role to play and do their best to help non-executives to play that role and to use their individual abilities.

DIFFICULTIES IN ACHIEVING THE IDEAL

1. The dismissive attitude that some chief executives and executive directors may still have towards the contribution of non-executives.
2. Constraints of time and knowledge limit non-executives' ability to understand complex issues, or to know the services in their district or trust, and therefore limit the contribution that they can make.
3. That the board have never appraised how they work or sought to improve that.

STEPS TOWARDS THE IDEAL

Some boards come nearer to the ideal than others, showing that improvements can be made by improving mutual trust and clarifying the role the board plays and the information that members require. All need to want to make these efforts work. The same general guidelines for leadership apply to the board as to other relationships.

CHAPTER 8

Leading in the regional office

'...responsibility will be delegated as far as possible to the level of local purchasers and providers, while maintaining accountability to Parliament'.
(Managing the New NHS)[1]

Regions in some form are likely to continue to exist in the NHS whatever further reorganizations may take place. The tasks of monitoring what is happening and of taking remedial, or, even better, preventive, action cannot be done efficiently at the head office of a very large organization. This is especially true where the aim is to have common policies applied throughout the organization The centre of the NHS is also too far away to know what is happening in the field, which is often essential information for making realistic implementable policies. So the question of regional leadership will always arise, though some may argue that with maximum devolution to the field there is no need for it.

IS LEADERSHIP STILL NEEDED IN REGIONAL OFFICES?

The abolition of the Regional Health Authorities has transformed the leadership role at regions. Regions are no longer independent authorities but are part of the civil service.[2] In their greatly slimmed down form *their leadership role in the field has been reduced,* as the quotation above suggests. *But there are also new opportunities to lead* in the greater opportunities for influencing national policy and to lead in particular policy areas.

The extent and nature of the leadership role in practice will only be discovered over time. Much will depend upon the evolving role played by the centre and especially by the nature of its requirements of the regional office. Despite these uncertainties it is worth trying to sketch what that leadership role should be in the longer term; what are likely to be the difficulties, and what steps can be taken to achieve the ideal.

In the short term there has been a considerable leadership task within the region in: merging regions, creating a new, much smaller regional staff, dealing with all the personnel problems from both these changes, and trying to ensure that adequate arrangements were made for the devolution of former regional tasks.

The argument for a continuing leadership task within the region itself can be seen even in the bland description of the new regional role in *Managing the New NHS*:

> The regional offices will provide a link between strategic and local management – a link which ensures that agreed national policy is implemented and which provides the information necessary for the NHS Management Executive and Ministers to carry out their functions.[3]

Studies of bureaucracies over the years have taught us that human beings are ingenious in doing what they want and not what they are told they should do by a central office. Hence, 'ensures that agreed national policy is implemented' – even if there has been consultation on that policy – is no simple task. Also, 'provides the information necessary' can only be done if the information that it obtains is not distorted. Yet the common reactions to the information required by the Department of Health: 'feed the beast' and 'ticking boxes' illustrate the problem. **Senior regional staff will need to establish their personal credibility if they are to be an effective link and relay point for information up and down. The previous history of regions in the NHS and elsewhere show that this is not an easy task. Because of this regions will still need leaders not just bureaucrats.**

The more detailed *Functions and Responsibilities in the New NHS* gave more idea of some of the areas where leadership would be needed:

> Regional offices will contribute to the development of national strategic objectives and will channel information and reflect the views from purchasers and providers.[4]

> Regional offices will contribute to the development of national policy and may take the lead in particular policy areas.[5]

> Regional offices have an important contribution to make in building effective communications networks.[6]

> Regional offices will...provide leadership to the public health function.[7]

> Regional office heads of finance will be responsible for ensuring adequate financial leadership locally, and for supporting national initiatives.[8]

The ideal

That the regional staff, led by the regional director and other directors, will:

1. lead by visibly demonstrating their concern for improving patient services and for the welfare of all NHS staff.
2. be trusted by the centre and by the field to understand their viewpoints and to interpret the concerns of each to the other.
3. contribute to developing performance measures that are accepted as meaningful by those in the field.
4. have the right balance between loose and tight in their dealings with authorities and trusts (loose is leaving flexibility for local decision-making; tight is controlling in key areas and where there are signs of trouble).
5. establish a relationship that enables problems to be identified and tackled in advance of trouble.
6. contribute to the development of national policies and take the lead in pioneering particular areas.
7. help to identify issues that concern more than one authority or trust in their region and where necessary take the lead in ensuring that these issues are tackled.
8. provide help in difficult issues of market management.

There are also ideals for the role of the regional policy board member that he or she will:

9. provide leadership to the chairs in the region and enlist them in helping to resolve problems where there is a deadlock between executives of their organizations;
10. adopt a similar approach to devolution to that of the regional executives.

There are corresponding requirements for leadership in the field stemming from the changes in regional role, namely:

11. chief executives and executive directors in authorities and trusts will respond to the leadership challenge of greater devolution.

Difficulties in achieving the ideal

There is always a danger of those in a lower tier of the organization viewing the actions and attitudes of those in a higher tier as being unduly constraining, and as showing a lack of understanding of conditions on the ground. There are two reasons for this. One is the different perspective that those in the higher tier necessarily have as to what is important, because a difference in tasks brings a different perspective. The other reason is that it is all too easy to lose touch with what is happening at the operational level and, if consultation is not adequate, to design policies and procedures that do not take account of the realities of operational work.

The transfer of regional staff from the NHS, with its own culture, to the civil service, which has had a distinctively different culture, represents a major change. How big a difference this makes to the behaviour of staff at region will depend upon the pressures to which they are subject, which will include how interventionist are individual Ministers. A more long-term influence will be the career background of those appointed to regional posts. Those who have experience of working in the NHS are more likely to be seen by the field as understanding their problems than those who have only worked in the civil service. The danger from a civil service culture is that the region will be seen far more than before as out of touch and not caring about patients, and hence to be circumvented wherever possible.

A major change in the role of the Department of Health and of the regions, like all major changes, brings problems of adaptation. Where the change requires, as it does here, a change in mindset, there are always likely to be *problems of learning to think in the new ways.*

The reduced role of region could mean that there is an even larger gap between the centre and field. Helping to bridge that gap is a major, and difficult, role for regional staff.

The difficulties summarized below are, at the time of writing, potential difficulties because the change in regional role is in its early stages:

1. **Ministers' actions make it hard, even impossible, for regions to adopt a light touch.**
2. **The Department of Health and the Treasury do not practise devolution** as intended by the review of the Department.
3. **Similarly, that regional staff retain old habits of intervention.**
4. **Methods of performance appraisal are seen as meaningless form-filling exercises by people in the field.**
5. **Those doing the monitoring attach too much importance to figures and do not understand what lies behind them.**
6. **There are insufficient opportunities for the field to influence national policy, and for region to play a role in this.**
7. **Chief executives and executive directors in authorities and trusts are too busy with immediate problems adequately to take on former regional roles.**

8. **Those capable of taking the lead at region leave in disillusion with a role that has become squeezed between an over-directive centre and independently-minded authority and trust executives.**

Two alternative difficulties could also arise:

9. **Executives and chairs in authorities and trusts continue too often to look to region for help with problems.**
10. **Region comes to be seen as largely irrelevant by people in the field.**

and a last potential threat to the achievement of an effectively working new relationship between centre, region and the field:

11. **Further reorganizations are imposed on the NHS thus introducing a new period of instability during which people are learning how to work in the new organization and are again concerned about the threat to their jobs.**

Steps towards the ideal

1. **Senior staff at the centre and in the regional offices are alert to the importance of 'light touch' and to the attitude of mind that goes with that.** Good contacts with the field will help them to know whether what they see as 'light touch' is seen that way by staff in authorities and trusts.
2. **The performance reviews are knowledgeable and searching** – the 'tight' part of 'loose–tight'. Good reviews require (a) prior work together on the subjects of the review; (b) an understanding of the issues and of the relevant figures; (c) a searching examination of whether the objectives, that should have been agreed in the previous review, have been met; and (d) mutual trust so that executives in trusts and authorities are willing to reveal and to discuss problems affecting performance in their early stages. The manner that regional managers adopt in their contacts with managers in the field will also help to determine how the latter feel about the region. The same applies in relations between the centre and regional offices.
3. **The views of the field on the utility of particular performance measures reach those who establish them and collaborative efforts are made to improve them.** A common criticism made in large organizations of the level above, and one often made in the NHS, is that central policies do not take account of how and why implementation may be very difficult, nor of what may not be done as a result. Unless

this is done the information supplied may well be fudged to give a misleadingly good impression.

Human ingenuity at ignoring or getting round regulations should never be forgotten. The answer to this is not tighter regulations but trying to get agreement on what are sensible and feasible regulations and targets.

4. **Communication with the field is seen by senior staff at the centre and regional offices as genuinely a two-way process, rather than primarily messages down**. For this to be possible there needs to be mutual understanding. The best way to understand the problems and attitudes of those who work in a different tier of the organization is to have experience of working there. This helps in understanding the different perspective that goes with a job at a different level in the organization. Central and regional staff can also learn by getting out into the field, taking a real interest and listening – there is an example of the power of this in Clare Dodgson's case study. For staff in the commissions and trusts it means taking trouble to explain your point of view and why you hold it.

There is a long tradition of meetings – often much criticized – between the chief executive of the region and the chief executives of local bodies, previously districts and now trusts and authorities. These meetings provided opportunities for networking and information sharing as well as for passing on, and interpreting, messages from the centre. The development of the new regional role, with much larger regions, and the growth of consortia for different purposes have made the situation very different from the past. Meetings between the regional director and chief executives in the region still provide a leadership opportunity for the regional director, but one that may not continue to exist, if chief executives in trusts and authorities prefer to set up their own meetings.

5. **The top group in the region sets an example of teamworking by visibly working together to a common agenda**.

6. **Regional staff and the regional policy board member help authorities with negotiating difficult decisions such as hospital closures or moves of major clinical departments**.

A different kind of step that would strengthen the leadership role of regional staff would be that:

7. **Senior staff at the centre often use regional staff to lead on particular topics**.

Summary

There is a need for leaders not bureaucrats in regional offices. The *leader-ship role* of directors in regional offices *has both declined* with the reduction in the role of regions *and increased* with the greater opportunities to influence national policy and to take the lead on particular topics.

Regional staff have a difficult task of acting as an effective link between the centre and the field. The *ideals* are too numerous to be summarized adequately. Their core is that:

● senior regional staff will be trusted by both centre and the field to understand and voice their concerns;
● keep the right balance between loose and tight in dealing with authorities and trusts;
● contribute to national policies and take the lead on particular topics.

The major *difficulties in achieving the ideal* are:

● too interventionist an approach by the centre;
● the top regional group failing to lead as a team;
● methods of performance assessment which are not accepted as meaningful by the field;
● too little understanding in region of what lies behind the figures;
● top regional staff who fail to lead upwards.

The main *steps towards achieving the ideal* are:

● developing mutual trust and two-way communications with the centre and the field;
● directors at region developing a team approach to performance reviews;
● knowledgeable and searching performance reviews.

CHAPTER 9

External leadership

'Relationships [with MPs] are built up, not when you are in a storm, but rather patiently and over a long period of time, when neither side is in trouble.'

(John Harvey-Jones)[1]

Many staff in the NHS have to work with people outside the NHS, other than patients. This requires two different forms of leadership. The first is to take the lead with NHS staff in setting and observing *appropriate attitudes to the local community*. The second is to *lead in these external relationships*. The latter can often be more difficult than leading staff because you will have less power to influence what is done.

The more senior the post, the wider the range of people within and outside the NHS who should be influenced. The main organizations, groups, and individuals with whom productive relationships will have to be established by health authorities and trusts are: CHC, social services and other parts of the local authority, GPs, voluntary organizations, various community groups, environmental health services, trade unions, the private sector, media, and MPs. The changes introduced by the Conservatives from 1989 mean that relations with GPs and the private sector are much more important than before.

The need for external leadership has always existed in the NHS but it has become even more important. There are two reasons for this. One is the emphasis in the reforms on public involvement and on the Patients' Charter. The other comes from the changes in medical technology which have to be explained successfully to the public. There have always been active opponents of hospital closures, but the problems that these pose for top managers in the NHS have become greater as the pace of change in the methods of delivering care has increased.

The ideal

You must know what you think is the ideal to aim at in relations between NHS staff and the local community if you are to take the lead in shaping local attitudes to the NHS. The following are suggested as the ideals that should be pursued.

That NHS staff will:

1. Accept that there is a **responsibility to account to the local community** for the service provided.
2. **Seek to understand public views,** and take them seriously.
3. **Care about the authority's or trust's reputation in the community** and seek to ensure that it has a good reputation and is known as a good place to work.
4. **Make the best use of resources in the community** that can help in achieving common goals.
5. **Practice an open style of management so that those interested in the community are consulted and kept informed about policy changes.**

If you are to be successful in leading your external contacts, you should pursue the following ideals in your relationships with them:

1. **Recognize your interdependencies and agree on commmon values and goals that you both want to pursue.**
2. Seek to **prevent or overcome mutual suspicions** so that you trust each other to work towards these common goals.
3. Having agreed your common values and goals **work supportively** to achieve them.
4. **Where there are differences** of values or of interests that **you will deal honestly with them.**
5. Seek to **understand** and take account of, **the roles, interests and attitudes of the other(s)** and the constraints to which they are subject.
6. Encourage voluntary effort and **treat voluntary bodies as partners.**

Difficulties in achieving the ideals

There are four kinds of difficulties. First,the common difficulties that arise when people from different organizations have to work together. Second, difficulties that arise from having to work with diverse groups who may have different interests and priorities. Third, the difficulties that arise from your own attitudes and those of other NHS staff to the role of the community or to particular groups. Fourth, specific difficulties that arise with particular organizations or groups.

1. **Common difficulties in relations between organizations:**

● The natural tendency for people to identify with their own group and to be suspicious of outsiders.

- Mutual ignorance of each other's work.
- External pressures upon one or both organizations.

2. **Conflicting interests of diverse groups**.
3. **Professionals' belief that they know best and that public views are uninformed and mistaken**. This may be true but it should not be the starting assumption.
4. Difficulties with particular organizations. Different groups pose their own distinctive difficulties in achieving the ideal. Those familiar with the relationship may be all too well aware of these difficulties, but they are worth mentioning for those who may later need to work with that particular organization.

- **The CHC** is poorly funded and has been called a 'watchdog without teeth'. Therefore, you should not overrate what it is possible for CHCs to do in researching community and patient views. Further, they cannot provide an overview of what the public wants. Long and Harrison's warning is still valid today:

    If the collective experience of CHCs since their inception in 1974 is examined it becomes clear that there is no such thing as a general public or whole population that is actively aware of, and concerned about, the wide range of health service issues that exists at any one time (Hallas 1976). There are many publics with specific interests.[2]

The difficulties for the CHC in speaking for patients are shortage of funds and the problems of identifying public wishes. Then there can be difficulties in the relationship between NHS managers and the CHC secretary, chair and members. These can arise because the latter feel that they are largely ignored by NHS managers and not given adequate information or warning of policies – in some authorities, at least, this is no longer true. From the NHS side, the problems may be seen as the CHC opposing changes (particularly closures) that managers believe to be necessary, or of the CHC not doing their job properly, talking about minor problems rather than paying enough attention to patient welfare. On both sides there will be differences in attitudes: some managers will not accept that the CHC has a useful role to play; some will, but may be critical of how well they do it; and some CHCs may be inherently suspicious of managerial attitudes. The competence of CHC secretaries and of members will also vary, as will that of the NHS staff.

- The **local authority** can be difficult to deal with because officers have to respond to the politicians in power. There will also be problems of the distribution of costs in community care. A further problem in some authorities is that more than one local authority may be involved.

● The main difficulty of working with **GPs** is that they are independent operators who value their independence and who vary widely in how they practise medicine. They have a major influence upon the health authority by: the proportion of services that are purchased by GPFs; their referral practices; use of drugs; and by their contribution to the authority's strategy. They affect trusts by the way in which, and the extent to which, they make use of them for their patients and by their willingness to change suppliers. They also affect the demands upon NHS resources by the attention that they pay to health promotion.

The reforms introduced by *Working for Patients* had two major effects on GPs, and on the problems that other staff might have in their relations with them. The first effect was the great increase in the power of GPs, especially of GPFs, when they became customers who had to be wooed by trusts and who had to be consulted by authorities. The second effect was the change to a more managerial approach to GPs by the creation of FHSAs, which remained after their merging with DHAs, and by the changes in the GP contract.

● Media relations can be a minefield for the inexperienced. The difficulties of working with the media will vary with the character of the local papers and radio stations, unless there is a problem that interests the national media. *A particular difficulty is that the media are often more interested in what is bad news from the point of view of the authority or trust*, rather than in favourable news. Another is that misquotation, quotation out of context and factual errors are quite common. Media reports can stir up local opinion, particularly against closures of clinical departments or hospitals. They can also arouse the concern of Ministers with difficult repercussions for local management.

● **MPs** of a different party from that in power can cause difficulties because they may want to make political capital out of problems faced by the local health services. MPs of any party may cause difficulties by supporting opposition to the authority's or trust's plans and by their reactions to adverse media reports.

● **Voluntary bodies** pose problems because of their diversity and the fluctuating nature of voluntary help, although this will vary with the level of organizational ability. Some of them may be pressure groups whose particular concerns may conflict with the needs of other groups, and with the judgements of local professionals and managers and with national policy on priorities. There are also problems from a voluntary body raising money for a particular purpose and then leaving the trust to pay the ongoing costs.

- **Community groups** can cause problems because of the intensity with which they may support a particular cause. As an American book puts it:

  > Sometimes community groups can behave like perfectly civil adults. They schedule appointments, make their case on the merits, listen to your side and accept a reasonable compromise. But not often. More common is the ritual confrontation, abuse and impossible demands.[3]

  Even if 'more common' is not so true in the UK, there are parallels.
- Relations with **trade unions** are usually amicable, but occasionally an issue arises that causes considerable concern amongst affected staff, leading to protest action in places. National grievances will be wholly or partially outside local control – partially because good local relations may help to minimize industrial action. Some hospitals have a history of poor industrial relations that makes life more difficult for a new manager.
- Problems with the **private sector** are likely to arise from the selective case mix of private hospitals, and from their diversion of consultants' time. The Conservative emphasis on increasing the role of the private sector in providing services, including capital, means that NHS managers have had greater experience than before of relationships with the private sector. Some may find this helpful in offering greater choice and in effecting economies, while others may still feel that the use of the private sector, especially for direct patient care, is a betrayal of NHS principles.

Steps towards the ideal

CLARIFY YOUR OWN VALUES

You must have clarified your own values before you can hope to achieve the ideal of agreeing common values and goals with your external contacts. They must also be values that people in external organizations will be willing to share.

Your attitude to consumerism is a major example of your values. It is possible, as David King has pointed out:

> to be in favour of consumerism without believing that consumers are always right and professionals invariably wrong, simply that they have some obligation to debate and reason with each other.[4]

Believing in consumerism means believing in the right of choice and of information. In a public service it means too that the public has a right to a say in the nature of that service. **How you view the CHC is one guide** to whether you really believe this. You should ask yourself how often in practice, whatever you say that you believe, you think that professionals know best and that there is no useful role for consumer bodies in a particular decision.

Your attitude to community groups is a parallel guide to your values. Such groups can be very useful, as two American writers (one of them formerly Administrator of the New York City's Health Services Administration) point out:

> they know, see and suspect things that even the best manager may miss. They provide a mirror...
>
> While community group tactics may be unpleasant, offensive, or just plain unnerving, it is critical for the public manager to remain object-ive about the merits of the complaints. Have they got a point? Why do they feel this way? What can I do about it? These are the questions that should be on the manager's mind in any community group encounter...
>
> Community groups represent your customers, and they are often right, or at least partly right, in their complaints. If you cannot accept this proposition, you ought to be in another business.[5]

Your behaviour towards the press is another indication of your values and whether you really believe in the public's right to know. How you react to criticisms in the press that have some justification is another guide to your values. One chief executive, who recognizes and accepts the role of the press, commented ruefully after an unfavourable news report on the care of young long-stay patients: 'the story made me a bit angry and a bit vulnerable, so it was quite good journalism'.

Your attitude to voluntary organizations is yet another indication of your values. The tendency is to treat them as supplementary appendages who are to be told of decisions rather than as partners to be consulted in advance.

UNDERSTAND PUBLIC CONCERNS AND PRACTISE PUBLIC ACCOUNTABILITY

The history of CHCs can provide general guidance about public concerns. Long and Harrison pointed out in 1985 that they have three recurrent concerns:

> strong loyalties for smallish local hospitals which can offer human-scale services; accessibility of services, including transportation prob-

lems in rural areas; and the level of services provided for the elderly, the mentally ill, and mothers and children.[6]

These concerns continue today.

These are a useful guide to the kind of criticisms that your CHC may make of new proposals and hence to the kind of discussions that you should be having with them. If your proposed changes are contrary to these values of proximity, human-scale and giving priority to the care groups named, then you are likely to meet opposition. You will need to explain especially carefully why you think the changes are necessary and to review what could be done to meet their concerns.

The main steps that have been taken where there is a strong concern for public accountability and for consulting the public are:

1. *Improved public information*. For example, using the media, producing a readable annual report and easy and attractive guides to using services and entering hospital, and providing information about the treatment and management of different illnesses. The latter supplements what doctors communicate, since they do not have the time to go into sufficient detail and the patient may not be in a state to take in the information when told of the nature of their illness. Since the first edition of this book was published in 1989, considerable work has been done to improve public information for both primary and secondary services.
2. *Surveys of patient opinions of the service provided*, originally pioneered 40 years ago by the psychologist Winifred Raphael. They are more common again, though they are only valuable if they lead to action to remedy criticisms.
3. *Involving the public in the planning of services and making the service more accessible*. The growth in the power of GPs and the greater emphasis on primary care are helping to make services more accessible and user friendly.
   In 1987 David King argued that:

   > the single most important step to be taken in making the NHS more user-friendly would be the general adoption of something like locality planning, dividing up districts into localities based on natural communities each with its own participative arrangements to involve consumer representatives in planning and service delivery.[7]

   Locality planning is now developing, though with more determination in some areas than others. It is a natural way forward though it is still too early to say how generally successful it will be.

MAKE GOOD USE OF EXTERNAL RESOURCES

To do so can require a radical change of attitude, perhaps by yourself as well as by your staff. This is less difficult when using the private sector since they are likely to take the initiative in trying to explain and sell their services to you. The problem arises more with the voluntary sector and with individuals who may not belong to a voluntary organization. It means thinking more broadly about what resources are available, or potentially available: asking yourself, or researching, what special interest associations can be used to increase or enhance the facilities and service provided. It means accepting that people other than professionals can help the sick and can promote better health. It means thinking both about what organizations exist in the community that could be helpful, and considering how to encourage their birth and development. The creation of self-help groups of various kinds is one example, as an American writer has pointed out, though the comments apply in the U.K. too:

> Increasingly, previous consumers of service are becoming providers of service. Their effectiveness is generally quite good. For example, groups formed and maintained by alcoholics, abusive parents, widows and cardiac patients, among others, have been able to support and sustain their members in ways which the professional community could not.[8]

BUILD RELATIONSHIPS

This is better recognized than it used to be with the stress on healthy alliances. However, John Harvey-Jones's advice in the initial quotation, of *building good relationships as a protection against later trouble,* is still relevant. It is an example of a general guideline that applies to many kinds of external relationships and especially to trade unions. There are more specific steps that apply to relations with particular organizations.

The first step to building good relations with the CHC, and trying to ensure that they can contribute to the effectiveness of the services provided, *is to show that you take them seriously.* This is true, too, of other relationships, but it applies particularly to the CHC as they may feel at a disadvantage because their resources are so limited and they are dependent upon the commissions and trusts for much of their information. Inviting them to attend authority meetings, as many now do, is helpful here. Members of the CHC can easily resent the way that they are treated and, like most other people, will respond to being consulted. The information that is provided for the CHC needs to be clear and easily assimilated since the CHC is composed of people from different backgrounds, knowledge and levels of understanding.

The media, and especially newspapers, need news. A recognition of that is the first step to building a good relationship with local journalists. If you make it easy for them to get news by providing press releases and press conferences when there is something newsworthy, good or bad, you can help to establish good relations. *The aim should be to establish such good relations that the news editor will phone to check any allegations against the commission or trust.*

Chief executives in the NHS have long been aware of the need to build good relationships with the local authority(ies). So this is unlikely to be neglected. The building of relationships at the senior level can help to keep each other in touch with emerging problems and intentions. Chairs who have a political background can often be very helpful because they will have more experience of working in a political context.

There has to be relationship building at the operational level, too. The development of joint care strategies for particular groups, such as the elderly, is one way that progress is being made.

Voluntary organizations are a potential resource that you may be able to use more effectively. You need to show them, and your staff, that they are taken seriously. If you consult them in advance of decisions about changes – for example, MIND, about changes in services for the mentally ill – you give them the opportunity to present the patients' viewpoint on these changes. You also enable them to say whether your expectations of what they can do are realistic. Further, it gives them warning of the likely repercussions on their own services; for example, more people coming to their day centre because of a closure of an NHS service. Accept invitations to speak to voluntary groups. Attend their annual general meeting to put across your current objectives.

More general relations with the community can be cultivated in a number of ways. A common one is an open day. This has the additional advantage that it can be used as an opportunity to involve more junior members of staff and help them to display leadership skills – good for talent spotting too. Encouraging the League of Friends by showing an interest in their activities is a way of trying to develop the commitment of those who have already shown an interest.

GENERAL GUIDELINES TO LEADERSHIP IN EXTERNAL RELATIONSHIPS

Leading NHS Staff

1. **Set a good example to your own staff, and to others in the NHS, by showing that you care about what the public thinks and that you are trying to provide a user-friendly service.**
2. **Set a good example, too, by the way that you talk about people in other organizations**. Do not talk disparagingly about them. Show that you take them seriously and seek to understand their views and problems.

3. **Be aware of your staff's attitudes to their external contacts**. Realize that some staff may be genuinely concerned to do their best for the patient, but believe that they will know what is best and that consultation is therefore unnecessary. They may be dismissive of the contribution that lay people and staff in other organizations can make. If you think that your staff's attitudes are contrary to your ideals for external relationships, seek to change them. You may be able to provide training that will help to modify their attitudes. An away day to talk through the problems of dealing with a particular external group can also help to bring out underlying attitudes, and to explore the reasons for them.

Leading in your External Relationships

1. **Be alert to what is happening outside** – that is, scan the environment where you work for possible threats to what you are trying to accomplish, or opportunities to further it. Such alertness is necessary in all management jobs.

2. **Be proactive: take preventive action to try to forestall any threats and seek to capitalize on any opportunities**. For example, consider in advance the likely reactions to a neighbourhood home for a small group of mentally handicapped people, and who might be able to help in getting a more sympathetic attitude.

3. **Develop good sources of information about the attitudes and intentions of those who can affect your work** – for example, know who are the people who really matter when you want to get support from social services. This means either building your own network or using that of others – some chairs can be very helpful here.

4. **Seek to get agreement on what are the shared values that underlie your working together and then on the objectives to pursue**; move on then to the specifics of who is going to do what by when.

5. **Learn to adapt to the different culture of the organizations with which you are dealing**. Be aware of the pressures that may divert those in other organizations from doing what has been agreed, such as political pressures affecting social services. Try to forestall these if you can, and build contingencies; for example, develop contacts with local housing associations to protect you against the local authority not cooperating in housing for the mentally handicapped or sheltered accommodation for the old.

6. **Recognize that in many of your external relations you are in practice negotiating**. Good negotiation requires understanding of what the other person wants – that is, what really matters to them, the constraints within which they are working and what you can offer them.

Whether you apply these general guidelines in practice will depend upon your values, how proactive you are, how good is your network of relationships and how skilled you are at understanding other people's attitudes and situation. It will also depend upon whether you are able to lift yourself above the pressure of day-to-day work and problems to notice what is happening in the wider environment. You can improve your leadership ability by learning to be better in each of these respects, hence the final chapter on Developing Yourself.

REVIEWING YOUR RELATIONSHIPS

In jobs where you have to deal with many groups in the community, you can find it helpful to list all the individuals and groups who can affect the achievement of your objectives. This is a check on whether you are ignoring, or paying too little attention to, those who could matter to you and to those who work for you. Next, consider the present state of each relationship, if indeed one exists, and where you should try to establish, or to improve, that relationship. Such an analysis is illustrated in Figure 9.1 for a chief executive of a health authority, though a similar approach can be used by people in other jobs.

Draw a diagram like the one illustrated and insert your main contacts outside the NHS. You can include both individuals and groups. Then rate each one from +3 to –3 for each of the following:

1. The importance of their support for achieving your objectives.
2. How far they are supporting them; examples of ratings here are:

   +3 = Already support them or are easy to lead in the directions that I want;
   –3 = Actively pursuing objectives in conflict with mine.

3. The amount of effort that I am giving to building/improving this relationship.

Summary

Leading in your external relations requires two different kinds of leadership. One is to lead NHS staff so that they have the right approach to their external contacts and to the local community. The other is to lead in the external relationships themselves.

THE IDEAL

That NHS staff will:

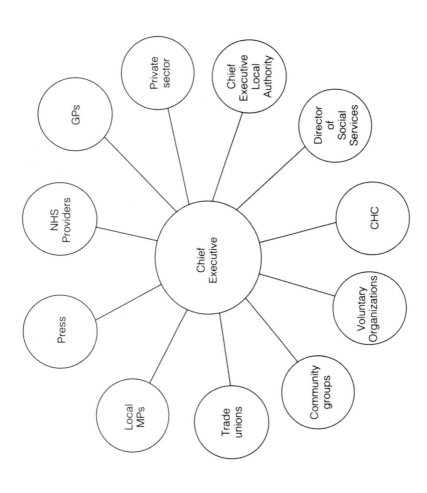

FIGURE 9.1 Network analysis of external relationships: illustrated for a chief executive of a health authority

- recognize their accountability to the local community;
- seek to understand public wishes and community health needs;
- care about the authority's or Trust's reputation in the community;
- make the best use of resources of help in the community.

In your relationships with external contacts you will:

- agree on common values and goals;
- seek to prevent or overcome mutual suspicion;
- work supportively;
- seek to understand their roles, interests and attitudes;
- make good use of external help.

DIFFICULTIES IN ACHIEVING THE IDEALS

There are common difficulties that come from working with people in another organization: suspicion of outsiders and mutual ignorance. There are problems that arise from having to deal with many publics whose interests may conflict. There is a temptation for professionals to think that they know best. Then there are particular problems in relations with individual organizations.

STEPS TOWARDS THE IDEAL

- Clarify your values. Your attitudes to consumerism, the CHC, the press and voluntary organizations will all show your values.
- Understand public concerns which, the history of the CHC shows, focus on the values of local facilities, human-scale services, and giving priority to the old, mentally ill and mothers and children.
- Improve public accountability and consultation in the planning of services.
- Make good use of external resources, which may require a radical change of attitude in yourself and your staff.
- Build good relationships as a protection against later trouble.
- Set a good example to your staff, and to others in the NHS, by showing that you care what the public thinks. Be aware of your staff's attitudes, and if necessary seek to change them.
- Be proactive in your external relations.
- Learn to understand and to adapt to the different culture of other organizations.
- Review your external relationships in terms of their importance for achieving your goals; of how satisfactory they are and the effort you are putting in to try and improve them.

PART III

LEADERSHIP IN ACTION

Introduction to part III

This part of the book illustrates how individual managers in the NHS, from different backgrounds and in a wide variety of jobs, *think about and practise* leadership. It provides practical examples of many of the points made in earlier chapters. Part III is also intended as a contrast to other parts of the book. Some readers will prefer it; some will like the combination of analytical chapters and personal examples; some will find Part III too anecdotal. The aim is to cater for these individual differences, since we learn in different ways. My hope is that most readers will welcome the combination because it provides two complementary ways of examining the leadership role.

Part III contains three chapters. Two of the interviewees in Chapters 10 and 11 were already known to me; one because she had been interviewed for the original edition and we had kept in touch since. The other examples in the first two chapters were obtained by asking my NHS contacts for the names of good young leaders in senior jobs. These were then asked if they wished to cooperate. If so they were sent the questions, given in Appendix B, and interviewed in person unless, like Nigel Clifford and Fiona Ramsay, they were too far away for a meeting to be arranged.

Chapter 10 contains four examples:

- chief executive of a health commission;
- chief executive of an acute hospitals trust;
- joint director of information services, DHA/FHSA;
- director of finance of a Scottish health board.

The first example is much the longest because it includes a discussion of the kind of community that the chief executive is serving, and of the implications for providing health care.

Chapter 11 illustrates managerial leadership by clinicians, and shows some of the new opportunities for doctors' and nurses' careers arising from the organizational changes. It contains:

For Nurses
- a two-part case study consisting of the original case study from the first edition, and a case study of her views in her current job as executive director – nursing;
- a service manager reporting to the chief executive.

For Doctors
- trauma consultant and service centre manager;
- consultant radiologist;
- two GPs.

Only senior jobs were included because they illustrate career opportunities: how the individuals have got there and what advice they have to offer. Regretfully, many other kinds of leadership jobs could not be included for fear of overweighting this part of the book. Apologies especially to physiotherapists and other paramedics, and to those in community nursing and in ambulances. Hopefully, they will find that much of the discussion and examples are also relevant to them.

Clearly more could have been made of leadership in GP fundholding, but for the fear that with a change of government this might date.

The aim of Chapters 10 and 11 is to encourage young managers, in all the activities that make up the NHS, to:

1. *think of themselves as leaders;*
2. *review their own views and actions* by comparing them with the other young leaders described in the two chapters;
3. consider what they should do to *improve their leadership ability;*
4. *review their career* and consider what lessons they should draw from the case studies.

Chapter 12, formerly Chapter 10 in the original edition, is retained, in a shortened form, because it is a more complete case study describing both the individual's views on his leadership, and those of his principal contacts. It is a case study of one of the district general managers who formed part of the Templeton tracer study of DGMs (see Appendix A). It is useful for presenting a very personal view on leadership. It is also of interest by contrast with the younger leaders described in Chapters 10 and 11.

Questions are suggested at the end of each of the three chapters to help readers to draw useful lessons from the case studies.

CHAPTER 10

Four young leaders

Case study 1

Clare Dodgson, Chief Executive, Sunderland Health Commission.

Clare Dodgson, who is 32, has had her present job since July 1993. Sunderland is an area of about 300 000 population.

CAREER

I had a very atypical career. I did not do any of the 'right things' that people traditionally do to get on in the NHS. I joined from school when I was 17 and started training as a laboratory technician because that would enable me to study further. I worked for three years but then hurt my back and was off for 14 months. It was suggested that I should leave the service, but I was determined that nobody would write me off. My parents were not in a position to give me financial help and did not know anybody who could give me advice.

I also felt angry that the reaction was to try to pension me off on health grounds. I said I was willing to be flexible as I could not continue in laboratory work because medical opinion was that working at a microscope would hurt my back. I went back in a very junior clerical job. In effect I had to start again, but was determined to pursue a new career in a different area.

I did nine years of part-time study while working, all at the University of Northumbria; first business studies, then a post-graduate diploma in management studies and then an MBA.

My earliest provider experience was in community health. I became director of planning and service development of South Tyneside FHSA. Then, when I was 29, I became chief executive of the Newcastle FHSA.

Both of the chief executive jobs involved major changes from what I had done before; the first one because I was accountable to an authority, and the current one because it involves larger-scale accountability, including a much greater financial responsibility.

I have not had experience of managing an acute provider, but I do not think you will meet any chief executive who will have everything in their portfolio of equal strength. Primary care has much more career currency than it used to have. A wide ranging experience of acute hospitals is not essential for a chief executive post in purchasing, but you do need an understanding of what goes on there. Similarly, those who have not worked in primary care need to understand the culture of general practice.

I got my understanding of acute services in a number of ways. I was involved in the review of acute services in Newcastle, when I was the FHSA chief exec: that was very educational. I also went to some informative programmes, like epidemiology for managers. My understanding has developed partly from contacts with clinical colleagues, partly from examining bids for development and partly from walking the beat. Occasionally I seek clarification of the clinical background to a particular problem, such as the implications of finding that a member of clinical staff in our local acute provider unit had hepatitis B. In my view the background on the service which GMTS (Graduate Management Training Scheme) used to give was very broad, and I am not sure that it would have been helpful at executive level.

CHARACTER OF THE DISTRICT

Traditionally, Sunderland had heavy engineering, shipyards and coalmining employment: that has gone. There is high unemployment and social deprivation with high levels of morbidity and mortality linked to that, and preventable causes of disease. Other problems like: a high rate of under 16 pregnancies – I think the highest in the whole of Northern and Yorkshire region – poor GP prescribing patterns and little interest in fundholding.

A district with these problems means that there are a lot of opportunities to change things for the better. [emphasis added] The northern culture of heavy drinking, lack of exercise, stodgy food and smoking all contribute to the health problems. They mean that we have to do a lot of work with the local authority, because many of the socio-economic issues in the environment relate very closely to what they are doing. We have been looking together at the Healthy Cities approach to address that.

A project in the deprived area of Pennywell aims to involve the local community mainly by addressing health, but also some social, issues. There is no GP in the area because no GP thinks he or she could get a viable list size – we have 13 different practices who have patients from this area. So there is a nurse practitioner in the project which is run by the local priority services trust. They work with parents on how they relate to their children. They also have community projects, such as classes for local children that are run by the mothers rather than by professional project workers, and a management committee that is chaired by a resident not by a professional; health visitors are in there trying to get across messages about immunization and family planning. It is quite a multi-disciplinary, multi-agency project. It has been worked up with the residents in partnership so it is *their* project.

Working in this kind of district makes me always very conscious that I am very privileged and that the professionals working there are also very privileged. I am also aware that the factors determining health are much wider than those that lie within the NHS and that, therefore, we must start widening our mind-set and think of more innovative approaches. You can't do the 'professional knows best, here is the information' routine and expect people to react to it, because they won't and in their situation I wouldn't either.

Trying to change people's culture is a form of leadership. But first it means recognizing the problems and priorities of the public you are serving, and making sure that the way you do business takes account of the reality of what they are having to deal with. [emphasis added] In trying to tackle problems like smoking, we have to be sensitive to all the other things that are going on in people's lives in a non-patronizing way, which is hard. As one of my medical colleagues said: 'If you live in poor housing with young kids, with all the problems that go with that, then concern for your health is a luxury item and to say, "Stop smoking it is bad for you, why don't you just stop doing it", is totally unrealistic'.

If you are dressed as a professional, talking like a professional, using the kind of language that we are all comfortable with, to people in a patch like Pennywell, you might as well be from another planet. They may well feel hostile towards you and will not listen.

I believe that people in the health service have many different kinds of people to influence, and that unless you can speak to them in their kind of language (in the broadest sense) you will not be effective. [emphasis added]

WHAT DO YOU SEE LEADERSHIP AS BEING?

The ability to inspire people and take them with you because they respect you. It is treating people as you would like to be treated yourself.

DO YOU THINK OF YOURSELF AS A LEADER?

I have to, but hopefully operating in the way described. The danger is that it can become an ego trip; rather it is a responsibility for other people.

HOW DO YOU TRY TO LEAD?

By example, by earning people's respect and by treating others with respect. I believe good team work is healthy. I try to lead from the front but not autocratically, although as chief executive there are times when I have to take the final decision.

I think writing memos should be the communication method of last resort. There are times when I try to communicate with everybody. For example, I led sessions for the whole staff about the formation of the commission.

In leading the merger of the DHA and FHSA organizations, one has to understand the amount of distress and concern that there will be and treat people like adults. You cannot say, 'I can guarantee you a job', or that this will not be painful, disruptive and difficult. But you can say, 'I realize that it will be disruptive for all of us, but the way that I shall try to manage it is to make sure that you all know what is going on and the process that we will be using to fill posts'. So that people at least know where they stand and how to raise their queries through the system, up to me if necessary.

There will be a lot of nonsense in a changing organization; for example, the symbolism of who is going to be in what office is so import- ant. What seems like trivia, like flexitime arrangements, can cause organ- izational mayhem. One needs good intelligence about the issues that will cause trouble: you don't get tip-offs about potential problems by iso- lating yourself. When you hear about one, a pretty senior person must be assigned to investigate and to sort it out.

I always try to keep my sense of humour.

I aim to run a happy ship, and although I may have a light touch it is not a soft one – what worries people most is when I say to them: 'Can I have a quiet word please?' If I want to criticize somebody I would say, 'I am sure you are as disappointed as me that this did not work out, what are you going to do about it?'

EXAMPLES OF WHERE LEADERSHIP IS REQUIRED IN YOUR JOB?

It is the whole job, especially managing change and taking difficult deci- sions; for example, closing a hospital. This means putting the case to the authority and going to public meetings to try to take people with you. I also had to lead from the front to bring the two structures, the FHSA and the DHA together.

WHO DO YOU NEED TO LEAD?

The people that I should most be trying to lead are those that I serve in the community – and that is hard. For example, trying to persuade people that there are very good reasons to close three out of five local hospitals is very difficult. This has to be done because somebody has to accept responsibility for the very uncomfortable decisions, where resources are finite and priorities have to be set. However, it is essential to take people with you, to listen and respond to their views and concerns.

The next group I most need to lead are my own staff. I am only as good as they are and I only deliver what they deliver. It is very important to me that they feel I am accessible and that they understand what I am trying to achieve and what their organization is aiming for. I feel very responsible for that and very aware of that.

The next most important group are probably the providers of services: the trusts and also the providers of family care services, the GPs. The interface between the two is something which I find increasingly important. *I do not think all of the service has necessarily recognized the importance of the interface, in that GPs and their clinical behaviour drive demand in the rest of the system.* [emphasis added] Too much attention has been focused on secondary care, and purchasing secondary care, but it is the impact of what is happening in primary care on secondary care that some people have not got to grips with so far. The trend towards primary-care-led purchasing should help change this situation.

We are managing the dynamics of that interface. We have to get across the message that we all operate in a system that uses public money, where resources are finite, and we all have to accept responsibility for that. It can be a difficult concept to get across, particularly to some members of the medical profession, although it is getting less so. I remember some years ago being 'torn off a strip' for suggesting that clinical professionals had a responsibility for financial resource use. Now my experience is that you get less of that kind of reaction from most clinicians, but there is still a sizeable minority who do not think that that is legitimate territory. I think one of the major challenges and opportunities is to get some handle on that through primary-care-led purchasing.

I believe that you have to start by targeting opinion leaders and influencing key people. You can also use incentives and, in extreme cases, sanctions. If, for example, you are putting in new specialist nursing services,we can agree that 'if you want access to this service it will be done in a particular way'. The problem with that approach is that it is usually the more progressive practices who will agree to it, leaving others in the same position as before.

I think it will have to be people like chief executives in partnership with medical colleagues going out and challenging assumptions, so that it is accepted that we all share responsibility for the best use of resources. Getting this accepted is going to be one of the big leadership challenges, but I think there is a national trend to greater recognition of this.

There is also a mutual leadership task with the chairman. Both parties rely on one another for expertise and judgement and share responsibility

for the performance of the organization. Ideally, the chairman and chief
executive should take different aspects of leading. For example, you may
need your chairman to talk to the provider chairman because there may
be problems that cannot be solved at the executive level, similarly with
the local authority councillors.

We have different parts of the leadership function and different lines
of accountability. Problems arise where the chairman is trying to do the
same job as the chief exec. I feel very conscious of chairmen also having a
strong leadership role with the non-execs on the board. I presently have
two chairmen: one for the DHA and one for the FHSA.

EXAMPLES OF LEADERSHIP ACTIONS THAT YOU HAVE SEEN

It is people who have managed tremendous change with integrity and
enthusiasm.

I have also learnt from negative examples. Don't treat people who are
working for you as if they did not matter because you are busy pursuing
your own agenda, because they rapidly get sick of it and stop working
very hard for you. I learnt that you do not get respect from your position,
but from the way that you behave. Unless you get people's respect, no
amount of hierarchical stomping about will get it for you! Working for
that type of manager provides a powerful negative example of how not
to behave. However, learning what not to do is not enough. You also
need a positive role model. I learnt from watching a woman general
manager, that you do not have to be aggressive to be effective.

A different kind of example was a visit from Alan Langlands. I met
him at a seminar and told him something about what Sunderland were
doing in primary and community care. He expressed an interest, so I
said, 'Why not come and have a look?' He came **and** had read all the
briefing material that we sent him; considering how busy he is, to take
the time and trouble to do that was very impressive.

He took a great personal interest in the individuals he met. I took him to
a very deprived area with a high crime record, vandalism and young
single mothers. He was interested, unassuming and he was very inspira-
tional and people still talk about it. The team on the ground were tremendously boosted by that. Yes, he was the leader of the NHS, but he was
also interested in what they were doing at ground level. As an example of
leadership it showed me a philosophy and approach to how to deal with
people, and how you apply that approach to particular problems.

DO YOU THINK OF YOURSELF AS A ROLE MODEL?

Yes and no; no, because it is not an ego trip and because I still believe
that, like all managers, I continue to learn from others. Yes, because if

you are in the front line post you are inevitably a role model. You have to be aware that people will be watching you, so you need to lead by example. I try to behave in a mature, adult way to set an example.

The more senior you are, the greater your capacity to influence people's working lives, for good or bad. I would not want people to say, 'if she came into the office in a bad temper, we all needed to be careful'. I would like people to say, 'she was a good manager; she treated people well and, as far as the senior person can be, she was liked and respected'.

I act as a mentor to staff, and have let it be known that I am willing to discuss assignments that people are doing for their educational work.

WHAT ADVICE WOULD YOU GIVE SOMEONE APPLYING FOR A JOB LIKE YOURS?

Think through very carefully the choices you want to make and be very clear what they are. There are things that you cannot have, or that are very hard to have: for example, if I had had a family in my twenties I do not think I would have got where I am when I did.

I am worried about women being developed in women-only groups as this does not prepare them for the real working world, which is not full of other supportive women. In my opinion women need to undertake personal and professional development alongside male colleagues in the same way as they will be working alongside them.

You need to be resilient, personally, and not lose your sense of humour.

ANY OUTSIDE LEADERSHIP ACTIVITIES?

There is not much space for that as I work 60 to 70 hours per week and sometimes more. In my spare time I try to have space for myself and tend to read.

WHAT HAVE YOU LEARNT AS A LEADER?

An awful lot: I have learnt the value of communicating with people and the importance of sensitivity to organizational politics. I have learnt how to stand pressure and not to take it personally. Research has demonstrated that there is a danger that women will say, 'it is my fault', whereas men will focus problems on other people or the context. One must not load that feeling of guilt on oneself.

I think that one learns on a lot of different levels. The academic work has all been helpful and has given me some theories and some tools that I can apply in real life situations. I also learnt some things that were quite stretching: new intellectual concepts that broaden one's mind and capacity.

I have learnt from other people: from the professionals that I have worked with, and from other students on the programmes who come from different walks of life. You realize that they do not take for granted some of the things that I do.

I have learnt a lot from my own successes and mistakes. You reflect on what you have done well, and on what you feel you could have done better: insight and reflection are learning. Like coming out of a disciplinary hearing and thinking: perhaps if I had approached it that way it would have been better, or that I really should have formalized this a bit earlier. Or when to speak out in authority meetings and when to keep quiet. Thankfully I have not done anything that has been catastrophic, so thus far I have been spared that form of learning.

WHAT DO YOU STILL NEED TO LEARN?

I will always need to learn to develop personal insight and to get feedback. It is harder to get feedback in a senior post but I try to get the team to do postmortems on how something went. In a senior post it is important to learn from experience.

I have learnt all the theories of good leadership during my MBA, but you must be able to apply them flexibly.

Maybe I could get a bit better at delegating, although I am quite sure that if you talked to my directors they would think that I delegate quite enough already!

I am also sure I could manage my time somewhat better. I sometimes wonder whether it is right to have an open door policy, as I do. However, I feel that if one of the executive board feels something is important enough to come and talk to the chief exec about, then I should be available to them if I can. I have come to the conclusion that that is a valuable use of my time, which has not been abused in my experience.

WHAT/WHO HELPED YOU TO GET WHERE YOU ARE?

My strong self drive to make a success of my second career in the NHS. I was also helped in planning my career by discussions with my mentor for the MBA, when I was director of planning at South Tyneside. I really did think it through then. Another influence, as a role model, was the woman chief executive of Gateshead FHSA, Jackie Axelby, who was very professional but approachable and had a sense of humour, which some managers seem to lose when they get to a senior post.

WAS IT AN ADVANTAGE TO BE A WOMAN?

No, though I think Opportunity 2000 has raised people's consciousness that there are not many women in senior positions. I have never believed in positive discrimination for women, because it is patronising them. But I think the service will be keen to have women who are the right quality, but not women as tokens.

It is very difficult for women. Personally I have not wanted to have children, but some women do very much. That is hard, as is shown by a survey that about 20 per cent of women in executive posts had children compared with about 70 per cent of men.

My perception is that the culture and style of the NHS is still predominately masculine, and in many respects success is evidenced in very male ways. Women have to be pretty tough to survive in that. You have to be able to function in isolation. I think some women find that harder than men. They want to be part of the team and to be liked.

My approach has been that if I want to play the game, then I play by the rules of a male-oriented world but seek also to change them whenever possible. They are very long hours if you are a woman with children. I had to accept early in my career that, if the job meant I was in before 8 am and did not leave until 8 pm then that was non-negotiable.

Because organizations are still male oriented, they are not changing to accept some of the priorities of women. I try to balance the long hours by taking a weekend to myself.

HOW HAS THE LEADERSHIP TASK IN THE NHS CHANGED?

Over the years in the NHS it has changed from leading the status quo to leading the tremendous changes that there have been since 1989, so the requirements of being an effective leader are very different now.

I have examined the work that I do and my time management to see if I could work shorter hours, but I have come to the conclusion that in smaller and smaller organizations, with the amount of work to be done, the hours will inevitably be long. I don't think with the changing management agenda we are expecting managers to deliver, that it can be done on 40 hours a week.

WHERE DO YOU SEE YOUR CAREER GOING?

I have no clear view at present. If I had a £ for every time I have been asked that since I got my present job, I should have three and a half thousand by now!

It is a very difficult question to answer. Partly because some of the answer is outside my control. If I see a job I would like I would ask whether I would be a realistic candidate, as I did for this job before applying. Also one may get approached to do something: who knows?

Case study 2

Nigel Clifford, Chief Executive, Glasgow Royal Infirmary University NHS Trust.

This is short because the distance meant that the interview was done by telephone.

BACKGROUND

Nigel, who is 35, joined what was then a directly managed unit in December 1992, as unit general manager of the Glasgow Royal Infirmary group of hospitals. Previously he had worked for eleven years in British Telecom in a variety of jobs which included general management, marketing and corporate strategy. Earlier he had taken a geography degree at Cambridge. As well as taking professional marketing qualifications, he completed an MBA in 1994 by distance learning from Strathclyde University.

He has had his present job since April 1994, when he was appointed as the chief executive of the new trust. The trust has a staff of 3500 'whole time equivalents' or approximately 5000 people.

WHAT DID YOU FIND MOST DIFFERENT ABOUT COMING IN TO THE NHS?

Firstly, you have to work within a different structure. That is, in the commercial world it is usual to have a line hierarchy managing the organization and implementing the decisions taken by the board/top managers. There are companies where this is blurred – especially 'people' based organizations such as consultancies and stockbrokers. In the NHS I have to be aware that decisions almost always have to be explained and to a certain extent 'sold' to the clinical community to elicit their complete support and implementation. While this is good management practice in any organization, it is essential within an NHS Trust.

Secondly, the NHS is clearly close to everyone's heart. Therefore there is a high degree of interest in what we are doing from patients, local health councils, local political figures and the media in general. Rocco Forte says of his hotel business that a hotel is 'a disaster waiting to happen'. So it is with hospitals, where treating over half a million people a year does test systems very rigorously and failures can occur. This can bring issues straight to me and my team which need to be addressed – perhaps publicly – very quickly.

Finally, in a longer established commercial firm one could take certain systems for granted. For example, key performance indicators, business planning processes and business case appraisal. This is not true when joining the NHS. A great deal of effort has been made across the hospitals in order to develop these and other systems.

WHAT DO YOU SEE LEADERSHIP AS BEING?

In the environment that affects us all, it means leading strategic change, setting direction and challenging the status quo. It means being committed to these changes and being seen to be happy and comfortable with the objectives. Visibility is important and so is setting an example.

DO YOU THINK OF YOURSELF AS A LEADER?

Yes, because at the end of the day the success or failure depends on the person in this job. The role is clearly one of leadership – setting a direction and energizing the organization.

HOW DO YOU TRY TO LEAD?

By articulating our goals, making it plain that national objectives like the Patients Charter do matter locally in a very real sense to our patients; engaging in debate with those in the trust and demonstrating professional integrity. I may have to challenge but I also have to facilitate debate, and though I take two steps forward I may also need to take one step back to make progress.

WHERE IS LEADERSHIP NEEDED IN YOUR JOB?

One has to stand up and be seen as the embodiment of the trust in public when things are going well, and more importantly when they are not going as well. In Glasgow we are having a strategic review of services; looking at this requires a balanced leadership, considering both the needs of the trust and the needs of Glasgow patients.

I also need to lead in setting the framework, criteria and processes for decision and action within the trust.

DO YOU THINK OF YOURSELF AS A ROLE MODEL?

I believe that this is almost inevitable in this style of job. You have to think how your behaviour rubs off on other people in all sorts of ways. Like walking the job and stopping to pick up litter rather than passing by. You need to be mindful of what you are saying and how you are saying it at all times.

Also, by demanding high and professional standards a message is given that we should all aspire to do our best.

Finally, as in any business, you have to be a champion of the customer – or for us the patient.

ANY EXTERNAL LEADERSHIP ACTIVITIES?

One insight shared with me by another chief executive is that parenthood is in fact an excellent grounding for leadership. My wife and I have children of four years, two years and one month. Thinking of ways to explain and how to manage disappointment and avoid conflict at home can provide some lessons for how to work in an organization.

WHAT HAVE YOU LEARNED AS A LEADER?

That you need to set the strategic agenda and not to get bogged down in the here and now, avoid feeling too comfortable with the day-to-day tasks instead of focusing sufficiently on the future.

Being able to say no, and managing the disappointments that come with that.

I have also learnt that on a personal basis it is important to me that the decisions made and the actions taken are such that I can sleep with a clear conscience at night.

WHAT DO YOU STILL NEED TO LEARN?

Having been a trust for less than a year, I need to learn how best to work within the board context and how to develop the various roles of chairman and non-executives. The discussion of the board is already becoming freer. I need to give a lot more attention to this new area.

WHAT/WHO HELPED YOU TO GET WHERE YOU ARE?

Three very good managers who I worked for in British Telecom. Jim Doyle was very good at fostering independence and had a sensible approach to risk taking. He was good, too, at developing team working. There was also Mike Read who had many of the same attributes and was also very good at making time for people. Finally, John Davies who I encountered as a new recruit to BT. He showed the way to involve people, and created a team with shared and motivating objectives. John was also excellent at making everyone feel they were contributing through giving projects, responsibility and his backing to people no matter where they sat in the organization.

Turning to what helped me. Luck plays a part in one's career. However, more constructively, being very professional in what you do matters; paying attention to detail so that your team trusts you. Once you have established this trust you can start looking at how you might help others achieve their objectives, how far you can support your boss and enable him to take his case forward. Come to him with solutions for problems that he may not have yet encountered. It is very important to be supportive. By doing so I have found you can quickly expand your own understanding and scope of responsibility.

Finally, as a junior manager, I made the conscious decision at 25 that I had to take my career seriously, and therefore present a professional face. It would have been easy to drift along without facing the need to focus on what career path I wanted. That decision led to a marketing qualification and a job change.

ADVICE TO SOMEONE ASPIRING TO A JOB LIKE YOURS

Listen and learn, particularly when as a chief executive you are usually so far away from the patient in the bed or clinic. Visit, listen and learn from people who are doing the caring. It is also increasingly important to have good presentation skills. I would advise people to acquire the base management skills so that you can talk finance, marketing, operations and information technology with the relevant experts. Practise thinking strategically – three to five years ahead. Think what you can do to make any particular job that you are doing stand out. Make sure that your documents look good, have no errors and are well presented so that your boss can pass them on as they are. By making him or her look good, you will also have some reflected glory.

HOW THE RECENT CHANGES AFFECT THE JOB

There is a profound difference between being the unit general manager in a DMU (directly managed unit) and being the chief executive of a trust. This is particularly true when as a DMU you worked within a health board that was used to being close to the detail. Now we have to come to terms with there being no big brother; we have to generate policies and plans ourselves and live by them. There is indeed a dramatic difference in a trust context.

The development of clinical directors as leaders of 'strategic business units' is an exceptionally useful idea, and one which is familiar in business. It should bring long-term benefits, as it should enable me to stand back from the day-to-day issues, though we still have to work at the education of clinical directors in business/commercial issues.

IS THERE A PRICE TO LEADERSHIP; IF SO IS IT WORTH IT?

It can be a very exposed and lonely place at times. It can also be a very stretching one in terms of time, as many people feel a right and a need to speak to you and try and present you with all their problems as the chief executive. Fortunately I have a very supportive wife. So there is a price. It is also worth it.

OTHER POINTS

We shall need to think about succession planning. Two out of the six chief executives in Glasgow trusts have come from outside the NHS so we need to think how we can grow our own.

Case study 3

Bob Grindrod, Joint Head of Information Services, Buckinghamshire DHA and FHSA.

BACKGROUND

He took his degree in English and Linguistics which included quite a lot of IT work (information technology), and he became very interested in computing. He went to Germany for five years as his wife was half German. He started by teaching English, and then became a management consultant because he knew both about IT and finance, and was bilingual. Because of the breakup of his marriage, he returned to England and joined the NHS in December 1990. He was idealistic and thought that he wanted to help something to happen. As a management consultant he feels that really you never own anything.

He had to come in at the bottom and joined the training department at Oxfordshire RHA to teach business skills. After two months this was taken over by the Oxford Consultancy and he was moved away to facilitate contracting systems. From this he developed an interest in purchasing, so he moved to Oxfordshire DHA as the business manager for the Director of Public Health, Dr Alex Gatherer. He started off trying to introduce a common focus amongst a group of very individualistic public health staff. He then became additionally involved in waiting-list information, and was promoted to be Head of Information for the Health Authority. A new chief executive to the health authority was appointed and it was a time of considerable upheaval, so he decided to move to his present job in May 1993 as it was a definite post.

It is an unusual background working in the NHS, IT and Information fields. People are surprised that somebody with a degree in English could be responsible for a half million pound IT budget.

WHAT DID YOU FIND DIFFERENT ABOUT YOUR PRESENT JOB FROM THE PREVIOUS ONE?

The environment was not as intellectually challenging as in Oxford.

I found myself having to fight for position. I do not like being in a situation where personal concerns tend to take precedence over the work to be done. I prefer to get on with the job.

WHAT DO YOU SEE LEADERSHIP AS BEING?

Courage; being brave enough to take decisions: there is a tendency to talk long enough in the hope it will be too late to take a decision. You need the courage to make a stand on what you believe in. You need courage to challenge performance management which is far too narrow, for example the excessive emphasis on inpatient waiting time for elective surgery as if that was all the NHS did. It is hard to have an intellectual discussion in the NHS about the merits of performance management.

You need the courage to see things through and to realize the vision that you have. You need a lot of stamina to really see something through and also to admit when you are wrong.

People can be very timid in the NHS. They are often afraid of saying something for fear that other people may not agree. If you speak out, you can help others to say what they truly think. There are a lot of senior people in the NHS who operate by making people cower, which makes people afraid to speak out. You have to learn to push down the feeling of fear, which is something I have only recently learnt to do, and to develop strategies to deal with those who would cowe you into silence.

The NHS is amazingly good at bringing about uncertainty. I think it has a long term effect; once people get into the habit of self defence and putting others down it is hard to change. I did not see that happening in Germany, where people seem to be more comfortable with each other.

WHAT, WHO HELPED YOU TO GET WHERE YOU ARE?

First of all, myself. Being self employed as I was in Germany is fairly tough, and the discipline of that taught me to be reasonably self reliant. I was also working as a management consultant with very senior people from German and Japanese companies. I learnt a lot about what people who are running society are like.

My boss, Dr Alex Gatherer, taught me a lot; to be more flexible, and that even if one is idealistic one has to bend in order to achieve one's goal.

Val Messenger, who worked as my deputy, was tremendously supportive of what I was doing and we did a very good double act.

One of my colleagues in the Public Health Department, Dr Jonathan Mant, became, and has remained, a close friend. He is someone whom I can trust one hundred per cent, and who knows the context within which I am working, so that I can discuss ideas and issues with him.

My work as a consultant taught me that it is the business that matters. It has made me very focused on why we are doing what we do in Information and IT; that is, focused on the outcomes not the machines.

ADVICE TO OTHERS

That is difficult as I have such a non standard background. I got where I am by serendipity. I was swept along as part of the development of contracting in the 'new' NHS.

It is important to do an apprenticeship for Information and IT, so that you learn to develop an understanding of the business that you are in. You also have to have basic analytical skills. One needs to understand the different priorities and language of, say, public health and finance. These are very different, but my experience has enabled me to converse with these different groups.

It is important not to stay in IT too long. The first thing my new chief executive said was, 'it is time we got you out of information'. There is a career ladder in IT, but you need to be careful as it is not the easiest place to jump from. IT people are increasingly leaving the NHS and coming back again as consultants. Indeed, people who want to change things are better off as management consultants, because when there are policy problems the habit now is to go to a consultant rather than to nurture one's own staff.

I would recommend working in the NHS to anyone, because it gives you a wider range of activities than you would get elsewhere: in industry the work would be more focused and narrow. There are also good opportunities to develop within the NHS, even though they are not very equitably handed out.

DO YOU THINK OF YOURSELF AS A LEADER?

There are two potential leadership roles; one amongst my Information and IT peers, the other amongst my staff. I do tend to end up chairing things; I do not see this as leadership, but I will take the lead when there is a need to keep things going.

When there is a need to speak out about something, I am prepared to do so and take some risks. One big issue at the moment is the national IT infrastructure initiatives, which are being very poorly run at national level: I feel it is better to challenge this now. There is also the problem that we work by piloting different aspects in different places. Something that might work quite well as a pilot should not necessarily be extended nationally. It is very easy for people to develop ownership of these pilots so that they find it difficult to discuss the problems objectively. I am prepared to make a stand and am getting better at knowing when it is worth fighting.

I see a mismatch between developing national IT policies, and the need to make better use of the information that is available already. It is a contrast between large national visions and local priorities, and with our resources we are not able to deliver both. There are some very useful things that we could do locally. For example, we could compare prescribing and referral data which could get GPs thinking about these two aspects of what they do. One can also compare deprivation with the resources given to different populations, and find that there is even an inverse relationship. There is a strange idea in the NHS that if data is readily available then it is not very useful.

IT is not the most obvious area to inspire people, because it is very much a means to an end. There is a vision wrapped up in IM & T (information management and technology), but one has to realize that it takes time. There is an evangelical role in IM & T in explaining what can be done with it. This is particularly true for the senior executives who tend to be 15 years older than I am; I am 31, which is just the 'IT gap'. They may feel threatened by it so you have to take on the leadership role of helping them to see what use it can be to them.

I would never say I lead my staff; I manage and develop them but would feel uncomfortable to say 'leading them' because of my principle that everyone is equal. I am not charismatic; I try to keep as equitable a relationship as possible. I do not see it as leading, but as being human; it is helping others to grow. There is an implication in leadership of being better than someone else. I feel more comfortable at the idea of leading my peers.

I would not underestimate the value of sometimes having a simple view of the world, a simple set of beliefs.

DO YOU SEE YOURSELF AS A ROLE MODEL?

I feel very uncomfortable at the idea of being a role model. I think leadership is enabling people to be themselves within their own frameworks. Perhaps one is a role model in the sense of trying to do the right thing; trying to be a decent human being.

OUTSIDE LEADERSHIP ACTIVITIES?

No, because I work such long hours and I have tried to dedicate what time I have to my wife. I cannot remember working less than sixty hours a week. There is a danger that one's work becomes one's hobby. You need to escape from that; I am trying now to refocus and work a shorter time. *There is a danger that once you begin to think of a sixty-hour work week, you let work expand to fill that time* [emphasis added].

I am doing a fair amount of mentoring of staff taking MBAs and open university courses; I am also trying to get people GMTS (General Management Training Scheme) places. This mentoring is a growing outside activity. I am trying to push people who are bright; I wish I had done the GMTS myself because it does give you an opportunity to look at the NHS from a wide point of view.

I would like to contribute more later: I think I am at the point of my career where I am still having to prove myself and in five to ten years I can give something back.

EXAMPLES OF LEADERSHIP ACTIONS YOU HAVE SEEN?

This is difficult because lots of leadership actions are day-to-day processes; for example, Alex Gatherer's abilities to allow innovative projects to happen. He had an ability to pick out what was going to happen and to get in early, by having projects to develop new ideas: 'risk management' and 'health promoting hospitals' were two of his major successes.

Another example was Mike Taylor at Oxfordshire Health Authority. He managed to change the whole of the top executive group. This made him very unpopular but he had a clear vision of what was to happen and his preparedness to be unpopular was important. Now people realize what he was trying to do. I think I could have learnt a lot from him if I had stayed.

Another example was Celia Richards who worked in Information and IT at the RHA. She saw early the danger of fragmented IT approaches stemming from the reforms. She was very tenacious as a positive focus on the logic of conforming to common standards. She did a wonderful job and started to gain widespread respect. Anyone who can actually see a project through to the end in a time of uncertainty could be seen as exercising leadership, because it shows to others that no matter what is going on there is work that needs doing.

WHAT HAVE YOU LEARNT?

Historically, I have been worst at being ready to admit that I do not know the right answer. I have had to learn that people with different perceptions may be right. I think it is part of growing up to recognize the values of other people's views. Fighting to get somewhere is not conducive to listening to others. I have started to feel that I am somewhat better at doing that, and to realize that I am not always right and sometimes may be fundamentally wrong; it is part of learning how to lose gracefully. Learning that, is the most important difference between me now and two years ago; I think it is part of a maturing process and my wife has been very instrumental in this, as has Alex Gatherer and Jonathan Mant. Alex said, 'sometimes even if you are right, being right is only the first step on a very long path'.

STILL NEED TO LEARN?

The ability to let go of things; to explain to people what I want and then to let them get on with it without meddling. My staff must find that frustrating.

Meeting new people and establishing new relationships gives one fresh opportunities to learn.

I also need to learn to cope truly with other people's aggressiveness; I like people to discuss things intellectually, not with a whole baggage of ownership, but that is naivety on my part. Again I think recognition of the problem is half the battle.

EFFECTS OF CURRENT CHANGES ON THE JOB

Stability becomes more of a virtue in this permanent revolution that we are living in.

One effect of all these changes is that you have to operate on a much more personal basis; you have to engage people emotionally in times of real uncertainty. Try to find out what their fears are. Management by walking about gives people an opportunity to talk to you and you can pick up the currents and try and tackle them. If what you pick up is *that their real question is*, [emphasis added] 'Have I a job tomorrow,' you can discuss it. For my people I am able to say, 'yes, I am sure you will be alright'. At my level nobody knows what is happening but I have enough self confidence to believe that someone will employ me.

OTHER POINTS

One of the things I do not like about leadership at the moment is the number of people who think they can get it out of a book.

One of my greatest concerns for the NHS is that in bringing in people with business skills there is a danger that they will forget that the NHS is not about profit. There are not enough leaders in the NHS who are making a strong case for a people-oriented health-focused NHS. It is important to hold on to your principles; I think I would leave the NHS if I felt I was doing something I did not believe in.

Case study 4

Fiona Ramsay, Finance Director of Forth Valley Health Board, Stirling.

Another short telephone interview.

BACKGROUND

Fiona, who is 32, has been in this post for eight months, and before that was acting finance director for a year. She started as a national finance trainee, and following her first substantive appointment has worked her way up in the same health board.

She works for a purchasing authority which has a small structure, with more senior people than in trusts. She is in charge of 15 to 20 staff; the complement is 20 but there are vacancies. Her job embraces finance contracts and information, so it is much wider than finance. She has not worked specifically in information, but her degree in mathematics and statistics was helpful. In the coming year her job will be widened further to include being the corporate secretary. The board has no special problems but is unique in Scotland in the geographical range of its contracts.

WHAT IS DIFFERENT ABOUT YOUR PRESENT JOB FROM THE PREVIOUS ONE

It is all the new contacts; working at board level one has more external contacts, also potential media involvement. This means that one has to leave one's detailed financial knowledge behind one and take a more strategic approach.

WHAT DO YOU SEE LEADERSHIP AS BEING?

There are lots of managers but not many of them are leaders. A good manager can run an efficient department, but a leader will provide the drive and the inspiration that will carry people along.

Leadership means being the figurehead for staff so that they see you; you talk to them and know something about them. It means involving them and feeding back to them what is happening in policy – this can be difficult in terms of time management, when so much time is spent in meetings.

External communications is vital; you need to create the external links for your staff.

DO YOU THINK OF YOURSELF AS A LEADER?

Yes, but with 'L' plates in this job because it is very different being in a substantive post, from acting.

HOW DO YOU TRY TO LEAD?

Leadership is also setting an example, by showing the attributes of equity, professionalism, honesty and integrity, and making sure that your staff understand this clearly.

WHAT ARE THE MAIN OPPORTUNITIES FOR LEADERSHIP IN YOUR JOB?

Leading the multidisciplinary contracting team in negotiating contracts to make sure that they are signed and they contain what is needed. Then there is leadership of the financial trainees; to give them more scope in their job so that they have developed some of the managerial skills which are difficult to exercise in a small team.

It is good to establish a reputation for being a good place for trainees.

DO YOU SEE YOURSELF AS A ROLE MODEL?

Yes, for trainees and particularly for female trainees, to show that if you stick to your studies and work hard you can get promoted to the top.

DO YOU SEE YOUR ACTIVITIES OUTSIDE WORK AS BEING LEADERSHIP ONES?

I am involved in several sports where, because of the nature of my work and because I am used to committee settings, there is a tendency for people to look for my involvement. Also one ends up taking the lead in a team if other people are not doing that.

EXAMPLES OF LEADERSHIP THAT YOU HAVE SEEN?

I have seen and learnt from both good and bad leadership. Bad leadership: I have seen inappropriate use of authority which does not give people an opportunity to contribute. People need to feel that they can have an input. By contrast, I have seen leadership which has involved staff much more. There is a fine balance to be struck because one still has to be the decision maker.

WHAT HAVE YOU LEARNT AS A LEADER?

To have confidence in one's staff and to learn to let go, and to accept that there are different ways of working even if they do things differently to how you did them.

To manage the personnel issues in a very changing environment with a lot of changes in structure. Helping people to adapt to new roles and learning to anticipate the kind of queries and problems that they might have; trying to minimize the disruption. I have also been working with an agency, and there are a great number of issues which have involved discussions with trade unions.

I have learnt to develop more confidence, particularly in public speaking. This has just happened; I have not had any training, though we are all going to have organizational development in future.

I have also learnt the need to try and make sure you retain your composure in difficult situations. I have had to learn to use my staff's detailed knowledge and to deal with questions that I have not anticipated.

WHAT DO YOU STILL NEED TO LEARN?

Being an effective board participant takes time, when one moves from the traditional finance role to the wider one. One has to be able to convey broad financial messages in such a way that they are understood.

WHAT/WHO HELPED YOU GET WHERE YOU ARE?

The training offered by the national finance scheme. I have always been doing work beyond my current level; at each stage the person I have worked for has involved me in more senior meetings, which gave me a lot of opportunities to pick things up.

ADVICE TO OTHERS?

It is a lot of hard work; one will be involved in a variety of professional settings so you need to bring more than your finance hat to discussions with clinical people. It is very much a learning process, and working with others you need to act like a sponge to learn how they do it and the importance of not using financial jargon. Presentational skills both written and particularly spoken are crucial.

OTHER POINTS

I think women need to learn to project themselves more; to make an impression and use their voice more.

Reorganization has meant that there are more leaders at board level than before; in Scotland there are now 70 trusts and 15 health boards. When they were directly managed units, there was a superior–subordinate relationship on the finance side as elsewhere. This is no longer so; some finance directors at health boards have had to cope with that adjustment. So that they are now dealing with people who are on an equivalent level, whom they previously managed.

Using the case studies

The Clare Dodgson case study is the fullest, so you could use what she says as a way of asking yourself the following questions:

1. In what ways does the kind of community I serve influence what I/we do? Should it do so more?
2. What lessons should you draw for your own career from that of Clare Dodgson?
3. Do you agree with her view of leadership? Why? or Why not?

Now, considering any or all of the four cases, ask yourself:

1. What struck you most about what was said? What can you learn from it?
2. What do they tell you about ways of continuing to learn?
3. What are the main career lessons for you?
4. What do you think would be the advantages of working for each of them? Any disadvantages?
5. What are the key lessons about being an effective leader?

CHAPTER 11

Clinical leaders

1. Leaders with a nursing background

Case studies 5a and 5b

These are two linked case studies of Heather-Jane Sears. The first is when she was Hospital Manager at Didcot Hospital. She was 29 at the time of that interview, July 1988. The second is of her views in a job six years later, where she is Executive Director – Nursing at King's Healthcare NHS Trust, a major teaching hospital in London.

Case study 5a

Heather-Jane Sears, Hospital Manager, Didcot Hospital, Oxfordshire.

Heather-Jane was young for the job she held. She was selected as a case study because she was unusually articulate about how and why she leads as she does, how she manages change and how she manages her career. She gives plenty of examples of what she does that illustrate many of the points made in Chapter 2 on Leading Staff. You will have met a reference to her in an earlier chapter on her views on the importance of being a role model for her staff in Chapter 3 on Leadership and Nurses.

After taking her A levels, Heather-Jane travelled around the world for a year to enable her to think what she wanted to do. Meeting people from different backgrounds made her realize that she wanted to work in nursing. She trained at University College Hospital, London, qualifying as a staff nurse in 1982. A year later she became an acting night sister and took her qualifications in intensive care nursing at Guy's. Then she spent six months in South Africa travelling around and working in field hospitals. Her first sister's post was in 1985. Within a year she became acting nursing officer covering Guy's at nights. She came to her present job, where she has 80 staff, in 1986.

Leadership

WHAT IS DIFFERENT ABOUT YOUR PRESENT JOB FROM THE PREVIOUS ONE?

It was a great contrast from a high tech acute London teaching hospital to a small hospital where I am general manager. Previously I had not cared for many elderly people, or worked in the community.

WHAT DO YOU SEE LEADERSHIP AS BEING?

A dynamic process whereby the leader influences others in order to achieve a common objective. I see it as someone taking the initiative, giving others direction, caring and sharing, not dominating.

It is the ability to enlist cooperation of people who initially are not keen to get involved, for example, the energetic staff nurse organizing a Christmas review.

WHAT ARE LEADERSHIP SKILLS?

Two-way communication: the ability to talk and to be understood, and to listen.

To give encouragement: some people need it and must be made to feel that their contribution, however humble, is still wanted.

Understanding staff's individual needs, like the sister who really knows her staff well, who knows who can cope with what. Everybody is very different and you cannot treat them all the same. It is interesting in general management because one has such very different groups of staff. There are the domestic staff with whom I communicate quite differently than with the physiotherapists and the doctors. They all have something to offer and they are all equally important.

DO YOU THINK OF YOURSELF AS A LEADER?

I have always thought of myself as a leader. I was always the ringleader at school, team captain, head girl, and the editor, and in nursing that went on. I think there are natural leaders: if you have a crisis there will be somebody who will come forward and take command. You do not have to be an extrovert to be a leader; you can develop into leadership.

HOW DO YOU TRY TO LEAD?

I am a democratic leader, but not laissez-faire. It is very important to get feedback from staff. You cannot really change things unless you take staff with you.

Integrity, fairness and consistency – consistency in mood and discipline – all are important. It is often these characteristics rather than position in the hierarchy that will command respect from those being led. I think you can really be quite firm and disciplinarian provided you are seen to be fair and reasonable, to listen to the other person's point of view.

I am quite a black and white person. I speak my mind. I have high standards and expect them of myself and of others, but people are individuals, some can do better than others.

I see myself as a change agent. I think I have skill as a facilitator. I will drip-feed ideas. I can implant ideas and get people to think that they are their own. I will pick off key members before staff meetings to implement change. I use my personality to sell ideas – people say that I ought to be in marketing rather than the health service! One reference said that I excel in the art of verbal persuasion. I was not quite sure how to take that. My father always used to say that I could sell sand to the Arabs.

Persuasion is part of being a nurse because it is an art that you learn. You have sometimes to persuade patients to do things that they do not want to do. Similarly you have to persuade and cajole staff into doing things rather than tell them.

A sense of humour is absolutely essential and I look upon work as fun. You have to keep a sense of humour, especially in the health service where it is very important to have a high morale. All my staff work extremely hard and they remain dedicated as long as the atmosphere is good and morale is high – that means giving opportunities, delegating, educating, being cheerful, caring for them, treating them as individuals.

People need reassurance and constant praise. They work extremely hard and everyone is ready to criticize – I remember that throughout my training as a staff nurse. They need praise to keep going, everyone does. – Those fresh flowers are from my staff. I feel appreciated and I appreciate them.

You have to take some very tough decisions. You have to stand by your staff's mistakes as well as your own. It is really important that you stand by people when the going is not good: that gives you credibility. It is that that they will remember when you leave.

WHAT ARE THE MAIN OPPORTUNITIES FOR LEADERSHIP IN YOUR JOB?

Encouraging staff, particularly in times of stress, for example, a primary nurse who is nursing a terminally ill patient that she is doing a good job, or a nurse who is doing a first teaching session in front of others.

The buck stops here: accepting responsibility is part of my job. If all else fails and we cannot get staff then I have to take decisions like shutting casualty. If staff are at an unsafe level then I have to come in and do it.

Being available for support: making sure that people know that I do not mind being phoned at home (behind her desk is a large sign giving her home telephone number). It is never abused, but staff do ring me quite a bit if only for reassurance that they have done the right thing, particularly a junior staff nurse if sister is not there.

Being a champion: I have to deal with the press, do a lot of public speaking promoting the hospital or explaining why we are shutting beds. If Radio Oxford turns up on the doorstep I am the one who has to speak to them.

DO YOU SEE YOURSELF AS A ROLE MODEL?

Her answers to this are given in Chapter 3 on Leadership and Nursing, pp. 38–9. She also said:

> As a figurehead I have to be assertive, it might be to the consultants with a complaint from a relative. It is often in front of staff so I have to be a role model. I think learning to be assertive in primary nursing is important.

DO YOU SEE YOUR ACTIVITIES OUTSIDE WORK AS BEING LEADERSHIP ONES?

I have always been the socal organizer for activities. I had done lots of fund-raising and that is very useful here. I joined the Business and Professional Women's group which involves public speaking. I was a national finalist for the Young Career Woman of the Year and so I got invited to lots of clubs to speak. I am on the branch executive of the Royal College of Nursing and also on the General Management Special Interest Group at national level. The Royal College has a national view of what is going on and that helps my work here immensely; it also gives me contacts for information.

Learning to speak was very useful, though I hated it at the start. It is very important for a leader, particularly in a community like this where you are the figurehead, that you can speak properly. If you are trying to get people to fundraise for you, particularly for the elderly who are not glamorous, you really have to sell it. It is important to be a good, moving speaker to do that.

I am very much involved in the community here. I run a carers' support group. I also get involved with groups that help the hospital. I have started an activity programme for our patients so that it should not be such a very long dull day. I have local groups and schools and churches involved so that we have all sorts of things going on here now: everything from animals coming in, to aerobic classes and pantomimes. That takes a lot of community involvement and it is very important in PR terms.

This is a small town, though it is growing fast. It is a community and the person they look to is the matron of the hospital. I am still seen as the matron. I am the figurehead here; anybody who wants to know anything about health will get in touch with me or write to me. It is the same as being the head of the police and the mayor – there are really about five key people in Didcot.

WHAT HAVE YOU LEARNT AS A LEADER?

A lot, above all I have learnt to appreciate my staff. I have learnt financial management, communication, time management and confidence, having to be the figurehead has given me confidence. People have looked to me as a leader so I have had to do things even if I am quaking inside. I always think I look calm outside: 'serene as a swan on the outside, yet underneath I am paddling like hell'.

I am naturally quite assertive, but I have had to learn to be even more assertive. It is knowing how to say 'no' firmly, and to give reasons why.

I have had to learn to delegate. Nursing is probably a bad kick-off point for this because nurses do not like to be seen as lazy. To move from nursing into management you have to get completely away from wanting to jump around. I always remind myself that I cannot do everything. Delegating not only gets the job done it also develops staff.

I think that I have changed as a person. I like to think that I am a better person now. If you have learnt to care for people more and to have a better understanding of them, that makes you a better person. Perhaps a little harder in some respects, I do not know if that is good or bad, but you have to take some very tough decisions.

WHAT DO YOU STILL NEED TO LEARN?

A lot, you can always learn to communicate better, to be better at time management. I need to improve my writing skills. The higher up the management ladder I go, the more I need to be able to write well. I need to learn about strategy and long term planning: in my next job I shall look for one that will give me more of an overview. It is very easy to get tunnel vision when you are stuck in the woods.

WHAT/WHO HELPED YOU TO GET WHERE YOU ARE?

Two people: my first ward sister at UCH, Joy Manger, and my senior nurse at Guys, Peter Brett – both were excellent role models for clinical practice and management. They made me realize that I had ability and potential. They made me think: 'gosh, if they believe in me and they see a lot of people, then I must believe in myself'. That gave me the confidence to apply for jobs. It is very important to believe in yourself.

All along I have applied for jobs for which I did not have the qualifications requested; for example, the sister's post I applied for said three years' experience and I only had one; I applied for this job after only one year as a sister. I had to put up with people saying: 'don't be ridiculous, of course you cannot be a hospital manager, you do not have the right experience'.

I am a very independent person. I left home when I was fifteen due to family problems and I have had to work quite hard. I have always taken a pride in my work, so I think that I have pushed myself along.

Career planning rather than job searching has got me where I am. I have not drifted into things as it is so easy to do in nursing: each job that I have taken has been for a reason. Nurses so often move sideways and stumble through their careers. You do not have time to do that nowadays as it is very, very competitive. If you are going to get there, then you really must plan.

I chose to be a night sister because of the broad experience that it gives you, I worked in every single area of the hospital. On night duty you are a much closer team. Because of the vast area you cover as a night sister, you learn to organize your priorities. One reason why I took the course in intensive care is that it is one of the most demanding; if you have done that you can do anything.

My area of expertise in entering management is not just nursing, it is very much personality, being able to deal with people. I have also had a lot of teaching experience. I have always been interested in teaching, counselling and dealing with staff.

My interest in people has helped. I have travelled a lot and met different people. If you have an understanding of people from different walks of life, that helps in your job.

I always try to turn negatives into positives: instead of saying: 'nobody thanks me' turn it into a positive to remind yourself to thank your staff.

ADVICE TO OTHERS?

Career planning: study your CV and recognize what is missing. If you keep your CV as broad-based as possible that will give you choice, because you do change and develop. But you must link jobs sensibly, so that there is a sort of direction which is not too narrow. You should plan to move just after the minimum time for that job. You should not leave too early as you must consolidate on your knowledge, but it is very easy to stay in a job too long. A year as a sister is the minimum because otherwise you leave the place in a worse state. I could have stayed as a sister very much longer, I enjoyed it, but if you are going to get on it is important to keep moving and to get different experience.

I am now considering whether I should move. I am quite happy here and could stay on much longer, but I feel that in any job you give of your best in the first couple of years when you have new ideas and you push and have a lot of energy. If you have a change then you push forward again. It is very easy to sit back after a couple of years.

You must look at your training needs after you realize what is missing in your CV. I did that. When I wanted a general management post like this one, I realized that I would have to manage the budget for the first time and that I did not have any financial experience. I was prepared to study and work at the same time and that means giving up things, also self-financing a lot in the health service. I took an Open University course in financial management. In my interview for here I stressed that this was a weak area and that I wanted and expected to have some training. I am taking the Diploma in Management Studies on day release, but of course I have to make up the time.

You do have to career plan, life is very, very short – it is not just a dress rehearsal. So you have to make the most of every day. It is absolutely essential that you seize opportunities when they arise.

Other points

HOW I MANAGE CHANGE

I had to change a lot here as it had not changed for a long time. I have gone on two speeds. There are some things that I thought were unacceptable: those I changed. A new broom sweeps clean; when you are new in a job is your best opportunity to make changes and I think people often miss it. The first stage in the job is absolutely crucial: you have got to find the right place to start. People will accept change from the new manager provided you are not too radical. I wrote down a list of what I wanted to change and starred the things that I thought I could get away with changing straight away, which was quite a small area. Most of the change has been in attitudes and has had to take place over a long time and I have had to take staff with me. Implementing change is picking off key people, convincing them and working it through.

KNOWING WHAT THE JOBS ARE LIKE

As a leader you must be willing to accept that you cannot know everything and must manage through people, but as far as possible you should try and do the jobs yourself. I am general dog's-body as well as being manager here! If we don't have a porter I will be emptying the bags. If we are short on the wards, I will be helping there. If we are short in the kitchen, I will be doing suppers. Which is good, because you actually are in the situation and you realize that you have been piling all that work on and you forgot the basics, like how long it takes the dish-washer to empty.

You cannot do everybody's job, but it does help if you have actually done it, even for one shift. You can understand what it is like from their side. It helps being a nurse; I understand the strains and pressures of being a nurse and so I can communicate much better than if I was an administrative general manager. I am very much a people person, I do not manage from an ivory tower, from an office.

MANAGEMENT METHODS

I use an action plan approach every two months. Eighteen months ago I instituted a system of individualized primary nursing care. We developed the plan for it together, and evaluate it every two months deciding what we could push forward and what is not working and should be thrown out.

I find it is good to have meetings with different groups of staff as well as more general staff meetings, for example, a meeting of nursing auxiliaries will say things they would not in an open staff meeting. I can then diplomatically feed these points back to the trained staff. It is better to have meetings when they are needed rather than as a regular thing. In informal contacts, having coffee with your staff, you learn more than you ever will in staff meetings.

I introduced performance appraisal for everyone from the top down. Untrained staff, such as domestic and catering, had not been appraised before. You have to educate them that it is really a personal development interview to look at training needs, not a slap wrists session. I am now working on a reversed appraisal system from the bottom up. Eventually the staff will appraise me, which will be an excellent way to learn on the job and as a way of encouraging others to be open to constructive criticism.

BALANCING WORK DEMANDS

Sport: I have to keep myself physically fit in a very demanding job. It can be very stressful, especially as I am by myself, top of the little pyramid here. Once during the last two years I failed to keep the balance between work and relaxation. I realized in time that I was getting too stressed, concentrating too much on the hospital.

I am asked to serve on working parties and all sorts of things. I enjoy that but they all take me away from here. You have to learn to say 'no'; otherwise you are out too much, and then one is not supportive. I think the main point of my job is being supportive. If I am on site whoever has a problem can come and find me. I am already away one day a week at my management training. Then I try to pop in first thing in the morning and at night. I am always here at 7am so as to have an hour with the night staff.

PRICE OF LEADERSHIP

It is really quite lonely. It may have sounded rosy – all my staff love me and give me fresh flowers – but it is not like that. If you have high standards, are trying to implement change to pull standards up and to stick within a budget you are not popular.

In my job I am professionally completely torn in two. Professionally I am on the side of the patient. I agree with the nurses and the doctors how terrible the cuts are. I will fight tooth and nail against them. But my job as a general manager is to live within the resources. You have to live with this tension. The doctors need to keep management in line, saying: 'what are we doing for the patient?' and the managers have to keep doctors in line by saying: 'we live in the real world'. It is a healthy tension, but a very stressful one for the general manager.

Professionally, I am used to making tough decisions: as a night sister deciding whether to resuscitate. You have to harden up. You have to be quite self-sufficient. You have to have confidence in yourself that you are doing your best. Everything is blamed on management, the whole morale and all the frustrations. The staff have to blame somebody: they cannot blame the patients, they cannot blame their colleagues, so they have to blame management. So you have to have very broad shoulders.

AND ITS REWARDS

It is a wonderful job, too, you do get praise. People do say 'thanks'. It is the appreciation, the little comments that keep you going. Somebody gets promotion and writes you a letter saying what they have learnt by being here.

I enjoy the job, I work for twelve hours a day so you have got to enjoy it.

Case study 5b

Heather-Jane Sears, Executive Director – Nursing, King's Healthcare NHS Trust.

UPDATE ON CAREER

In 1989, I left Didcot Hospital to take on the challenge of a dual role, as regional nurse/policy analyst for Oxford Region. Half of the post was funded by Cancer Relief Macmillan Fund (CRMF), with the remit to develop and co-ordinate palliative care services across the four counties of Northamptonshire, Buckinghamshire, Oxfordshire and Berkshire.

The other half of my role encompassed service and capital planning in its broadest sense – from functional suitability studies and option appraisals, to major incident planning. Working closely with the directorate of public health broadened my thinking on needs analysis and clinical effectiveness. I also developed my political skills and understanding of the relationship between the government and Department of Health.

The NHS reforms opened up a choice of career paths for me; I had worked at region in needs analysis and strategic planning, but the initially immature state of the 'market' did not make purchasing an attractive option at that time. The power then, was in providing, and the new freedoms offered to trusts were attracting bright leaders who wanted to challenge the status quo. I wanted to be part of the action and seized the opportunity to take on what I knew would be a challenging and high profile role.

I was delighted to be approached for the job of Executive Director – Nursing at the King's Healthcare NHS Trust , and certainly do not regret my decision to accept.

I have particularly enjoyed the dual nature of the role, not only the professional leadership, but also as a general manager, playing a central part in turning the organization around.

I lead the following strategies:

- Nursing & midwifery;
- Continuous quality improvement;
- Health of the Nation;
- Corporate communications.

Since 1986, I have also completed an Open University course in finance and accounting; a diploma in management studies; an international diploma in marketing; and an international masters degree in business administration.

In addition, I have contributed to a variety of consultancy projects, including visits to Malaysia, Russia, Canada, and the USA.

REREADING THE PREVIOUS CASE STUDY WHAT COMMENTS DO YOU WANT TO MAKE? IS THERE ANYTHING THAT YOU NOW DISAGREE WITH OR WANT TO MODIFY?

Some of the English – which has been done in this edition – and the naivety! A lot has happened in the last six years.

I spoke about encouraging *some* people – in retrospect I do not know why I added 'some' – *everyone* needs encouragement, and a leader can never underestimate the power of giving sincere positive feedback.

When asked about how I try to lead, I talked about my values of integrity, fairness and consistency – I would like to add honesty (after integrity) – people need to know the facts and how the team/organization stands in relation to them. An honest and fair relationship is crucial in successful coaching, and mentorship.

I also spoke of taking some tough decisions – I did, but in the context of the change agenda that we have managed at King's during the last three years, they rather pale into insignificance! Post Tomlinson, we have closed peripheral hospitals, lost community services and downsized from 6000 to 4000 members of staff.

I spoke about being a champion and having to deal with the press. In my current role, I wear the additional hat of director of corporate communications, dealing with a wide range of media enquiries and television crews. I have also learnt a lot about dealing with journalists from my chief executive, as it is one of his many strengths.

Acting as a role model is still important to me. Although I am no longer in clinical practice, I do three or four 'ward rounds' every week, speaking to patients, visitors, and members of staff from all levels and disciplines. This helps to keep me in touch, and offers the opportunity to question and challenge current practice. For example, concerning confidentiality, privacy and dignity, or the scope of professional practice – checking that staff appreciate the value of research-based practice, and really understand the concept of professional accountability.

I emphasize the importance of critical thinking and encourage staff to present their solutions to problems cogently. It is easy for clinical staff, at the sharp end of patient care, to lose battles through straying, emotionally from the point of the argument. I try to facilitate a problem solving approach that gets them to articulate the benefits and concerns around issues. This more focused approach helps to channel negative energy into positive thinking – after all, it is usually the people at 'grass roots', who come up with the most creative solutions.

When asked about my 'management methods' I spoke of being action orientated and managing by objectives – if anything, I have become more convinced of this approach. With the huge change agenda facing us all, it is so easy for people to get side-tracked and spend unproductive time on peripheral issues. I have developed a loose–tight style of managing my team through explicit objectives, with mutually agreed success criteria – I give a lot of freedom for them to choose how they approach tasks, but expect regular variance reports if they have reason to stray from agreed timescales or outcomes.

I am fortunate in that I have made some excellent appointments – members of the team need little management, just occasional coaching, and plenty of encouragement.

People can not really be *managed* anyway. Inventories can be managed, but people are usually *led*.

I was interested to read the case study again – I encourage reflective practice and know its value in personal development. However, it is an area that I am not very disciplined in myself – not formally anyway. I always try to focus on the best and the worst thing that happens every day, as I drive home – trying to learn from experience and decide how I would do things differently if I ever found myself in a similar situation. Often, I have an incredibly packed day – rich in learning opportunities – it is then that I really should spend time writing a reflective diary, but no sooner than I have thought about it, I am on to the next thing, and the opportunity has passed.

Reading the case study helped me to reflect on how valuable my general management experience at Didcot was – it seems incredible that there are so many parallels, with the management of change at King's. You would not think so comparing a unit of 30 beds and a turnover of £450 000 with one of 880 beds and a turnover in excess of £140m, but I guess the principles are just the same.

IN YOUR JOB IN THE EARLIER INTERVIEW YOU WERE A HANDS-ON LEADER. IS THAT POSSIBLE, IN YOUR PRESENT JOB?

Not really – my diary is packed.

Yet I certainly miss clinical practice and the benefits of hands-on leadership would be twofold: firstly, it would be easier to maintain credibility with ward staff; secondly, it would increase the opportunity for 'grass roots' communication – keeping me in touch with the views of patients, visitors and staff.

I believe that I can also remain credible as a leader by exhibiting my broader knowledge base of health care management, and in particular keeping myself up to date and well briefed on research-based practice issues, such as clinical effectiveness and outcomes.

This also takes time of course – a good network of experts, and the ability to sort critically and to speed-read journals is essential.

NEW FORMS OF LEADERSHIP IN YOUR PRESENT JOB?

I have moved from operational management to a position of strategic influence. This calls for skill, confidence, patience and resilience.

Skill in understanding the intricacies of informal power in a complex organization. Only by building relationships and getting to grips with what motivates those with power and what you can trade with them, can you really begin to exert sufficient influence to make things happen.

Confidence in yourself and your team, enabling you to take risks when standing up for what you believe and want. For example, presenting a controversial paper to the trust board, or negotiating an increase in resources with the executive.

Patience in waiting for the 'echo factor' – drip feeding ideas, until they come back as someone else's! Working through influence can be frustrating because you usually have to work harder and wait longer before you can appreciate the results.

Resilience in coping with the stress of political infighting, and cultural power struggles between key players – it happens in most organizations, but it can be very wearing. You also need tremendous energy and commitment to succeed given the long hours, excessive paperwork, and continual rise in expectations.

OF HELP TO ME AND WAYS OF LEARNING

There are five things:

(1) *Personal* – I have an extremely bright, understanding and supportive husband, to whom I owe a great deal. We have two delightful daughters who not only provide a balance in life, but also ask challenging questions like 'why?'!

(2) *Colleagues* – I have enjoyed building a varied and complementary team, and it never ceases to amaze me how hard they all work. As long as they continue to challenge me, I will keep my feet on the ground – you need that – nobody wants to become a megalomaniac!

(3) *Networking* – I have always believed in keeping in touch with a wide range of interesting people. It is easy to become inward looking in large organizations, but one must always make time to get objective views from outside. People from different backgrounds may have a fresh approach.

(4) *Shadowing* – I also believe that occasional shadowing of other managers can help to put problems into perspective, and provide an opportunity for fresh thinking and creativity. It also helps you to understand other people's organizations, roles and leadership styles.

(5) *Project Management* – I have recently set up an exchange scheme for nurses/midwives wishing to gain experience in purchasing/providing. We use an action learning approach, enabling people to carry out projects that are of use to the host organization – this has proved successful, and is more cost effective than shadowing and taught courses.

(6) *Advice to others* – As regards continual learning, I can not really beat Tom Peters, who said: 'The person who sees a career as one of perpetual investment in education, stands a much better chance of surviving in today's world'.

MANAGEMENT METHODS

I have already mentioned my preference for management by walking about (MBWA), and also my approach to exception reporting in performance management.

I try to inspire, challenge and encourage people to take risks – this requires confidence and the ability to establish close working relationships with team members. Only by building credibility and trust, can you truly coach and offer supportive development opportunities.

I am also known for the following phrases:

- *'Go for it – before someone else does'* – given that there is no such thing as original thought, good ideas need to be turned into action *fast*.
- *'Quality not Quantity'* – my team call me 'Two Sides Max'! It helps to focus ideas, cuts down on the amount of reading everyone has, and saves trees.
- *'Don't agonize – organize!'* – if I have a problem, I try to solve it quickly and move on, as a role model to my team.
- *'Fun fights fatigue'* – it really does help to be part of a team with a sense of humour. We should all strive to inject more fun and enjoyment into work, it helps release pressure and combats stress.
- *'Golden Grains'* – this is a theory that I have had for many years, but somehow it seems even more pertinent to an executive position, where one rarely has positive feedback or thanks (in comparison to those with direct patient contact). When I get a particularly nice call, note or card from someone in appreciation, I put it away with a mental bag of other 'golden grains', to sift through on dark evenings when things have been tough. In other words, cherish the thanks, they can be few and far between – no one chooses to become a manager to be popular.

BALANCING WORK DEMANDS

Difficult! I pride myself on good time management and still get it wrong from time to time – especially just before a holiday, when I know that I am running on empty, and not clearing the desk as efficiently as I should.

I have already mentioned my supportive husband, who is a real saint and even tolerates my paperwork on Sunday afternoons. I would like to say that I only work 08.00 to 17.00 and never take work home at weekends, but unfortunately it just is not true. I am getting better, but it is sometimes a struggle – if you know of anyone in the NHS who has cracked it, please put them in touch!

I am however disciplined with our social life – I have always believed in working and playing hard, with sport, entertaining, and plenty of relaxing breaks abroad, which I enter into my diary at the start of the year.

PRICE OF LEADERSHIP

Hard work and less than optimum time with the family. I am also not as fit as I would like to be – there are still many late meetings, preventing regular trips to the health club. It is also difficult to find time to reflect on and evaluate decisions. I would like, for example, to explore the impact of leadership and management decisions on clinical effectiveness, as a PhD in organizational development.

AND ITS REWARDS

I still believe passionately in the NHS and what we are trying to achieve. I enjoy leadership and the power to change things for the better.

My greatest pleasure remains in coaching and developing staff – their achievements and progression are what continue to motivate and sustain my enthusiasm.

Case study 6

Olga Senior, Service Manager, Radcliffe Infirmary NHS Trust, Oxford

Olga was 34 when interviewed in early 1995. She joined the NHS in 1978, straight from school, originally as a nursing auxiliary. During her nurse training in Oxford she decided that she wanted to do theatre nursing. Her first staff nurse post was in theatres at the Radcliffe Infirmary, specializing in plastic surgery. In 1983, she married and moved to Bristol. She did a post-registration course in theatre nursing. After working for some months in the children's hospital in Bristol, the senior consultant in plastic surgery at the Radcliffe Infirmary approached her about a vacancy for a theatre sister, insisting that it was a Monday to Friday job. She attended an interview and was successful. She stayed in that job for three and a half years.

For eighteen months she continued to live in Bristol and commuted to Oxford. In retrospect she thought this was a good thing, because you could not mix work with your social life. Her husband then obtained a job in London so they decided to live in Oxford.

She won the Smith and Nephew theatre nurse scholarship which enabled her to go and work in America for three months, studying theatre nursing in Louisville, Kentucky and Baltimore and to look at other things as well.

In 1988 the opportunity came to work with the assistant transplant co-ordinator at the Oxford region. Her aim was to look at what was happening outside theatres. She also wanted to learn skills she did not have: presentation and counselling bereaved people. After a year she felt she had achieved those objectives and applied for the senior nurse job in plastic surgery at the Radcliffe Infirmary, but with a bit of trepidation because she had not done any ward nursing.

In 1990 she was offered a six months secondment to business management. During that time she felt that she had found her niche, soon realizing that nursing was only a small part of the NHS and that perhaps this job was the way to make things better for the patients – to know about patient care but to be removed from it. At the end of the six months, she got a newly created business management post, covering plastic surgery, neurosurgery and diabetes. In the latter part of 1991 there was a further change in the structure which created two service managers' posts. She applied for the surgical service manager's post and has held it since September 1991.

MAJOR DIFFERENCES BETWEEN NURSING AND YOUR PRESENT JOB?

The span of people that I interact with: when I was nursing it was the medical staff, patients and relatives. Now it is those groups plus nursing staff, finance, NHS purchasers and GPs. *Talking to a much wider span of people enables you to make changes happen across a wider field. If you get it right you can change how services are delivered.* [emphasis added]

There is a sense of satisfaction [emphasis added]: I manage ENT, ophthalmology, neurosurgery and plastic surgery, which is half of the Radcliffe Infirmary, £15 million+ budget. Ophthalmology is a huge service; when I started in 1991 the only feedback from GPs was: 'what an awful service'. It is still not completely right, but it is a different service from 1991. I have not done it alone, but there are some parts of it that I have thought up and implemented which is satisfying.

My only regret is: 'should I have made the move from nursing earlier?' I love it now because you seem to be able to encompass the whole of it.

DO YOU THINK OF YOURSELF AS A LEADER?

I think that I am both a leader and a manager of the surgical services. This job is a pivotal role because most clinicians want to be looking after patients. It means having the overall view and facilitating and enabling. Patient care would continue if I was not in post but I do think I am improving services. My role is to ensure that everything that is needed is in place.

I am very glad that we have 'service manager' rather than 'business manager', because I lead a service. Clinicians should not be bothered with all the minutiae. The consultants and I fight at times, but in a healthy way, about what is good for patients. There is a very healthy relationship between doctors and managers at the Radcliffe Infirmary.

I like working with different people and I like people, I like to lead.

HOW DO YOU TRY TO LEAD?

A leader needs to have ideas: people do look to the leader to create ideas, that is to have a vision and to move the services on. There are the areas that you see could be better and then you need to win people's hearts and minds and convince them of the changes required. You need to try and get the idea of change to be theirs, by sowing ideas. You should also be making the difficult decisions when other people do not want to make them.

Leadership is providing stability, David Wilson (Chief Executive) has been here for 14 years and I have been in post for four years. It is unusual for people to stay in such a post for four years yet I can still see another four years work. You only learn from experience what matters and you cannot learn that from a textbook, so it is good to stay in the same job, but it begins with all these movements to look odd if you do stay put. I have said: 'do tell me if you think I am running out of steam'. Perhaps people do not want to stay in the same job for fear that their mistakes will catch up with them!

DO YOU THINK OF YOURSELF AS A ROLE MODEL?

Yes, of what a manager is like to: consultants, other managers, the assistant clinical manager and perhaps to other clerical and administrative staff too, and also to patients. For example, if there is a problem in outpatients I tell them to call for me, and you can sometimes defuse it before it becomes a real issue.

I also see myself as a role model by being authoritative and being in authority: my post is where the buck stops. There are some issues that I would see as my responsibility and others I would see as joint with the chief executive.

OUTSIDE LEADERSHIP ACTIVITIES?

Yes, I was a school prefect and head girl and I am very active in the old girls' association. Anything I am involved in, I think I am the same. I do not mind taking a leadership role and people tend to look to me to do that.

WHAT DO YOU FEEL YOU HAVE LEARNED AS A LEADER?

Patience, things do take a long time to actually happen. One may feel that I could have done it quicker myself, but I believe in letting people implement their own ideas, even if it means they have to find out for themselves.

I have learnt that role models are important, one of the pluses as you go up the tree is to pick the best of various people and put them together.

I do try and work through others but I have learnt there are some things where you will not get consensus and one learns to recognize these.

As a leader you have to be consistent in what you are saying, the people you are leading quickly find your inconsistencies.

Another thing I have learnt is saying, 'I think I have got this wrong', but saying it in a way that you do not lose respect.

WHAT DO YOU STILL NEED TO LEARN?

More patience, I do not think you ever stop learning. In 1991 there was often something new, now there is always something new, but quite a bit you base on experience.

There are a few skills that I have to improve, like finance. I have got to learn to finish things off and be more focused: if the phone rings and a clinician says he has a problem in his outpatients department, I will go out, then I am approached about other things and I never get back to my desk. Then you cannot lead effectively because you are so bogged down.

Delegation is another skill I need to improve on, but I think you need the right structure around you, and continue to learn how it all fits together.

WHO HELPED YOU TO GET WHERE YOU ARE?

David Wilson as CE of the Radcliffe Infirmary, the stability that he has created by being there for many years. He has been able to assess what I could achieve and encouraged me to go for it. Mary Hodgson, the director of nursing, persuaded me to make the career change from nursing to management. I went through some agony about that change, but it was very helpful to have someone say to me: 'it is time to move on'. The third person who helped was the tutor in nursing at the John Radcliffe hospital who took me through a short one-week course on the management of change, on which I learnt so much and always remember.

WHAT ADVICE WOULD YOU GIVE TO SOMEONE ASPIRING TO A JOB LIKE YOURS?

As one gets to a senior post in the NHS it is a strength to have had health service experience so that you understand how a hospital works. It is also helpful to have worked at different levels so that you understand how the different bits fit together. Our chair, who comes from outside the NHS, has sought to learn how the hospital works by working for a day in different kinds of jobs, like the switchboard.

One needs to be a clear thinker so as to understand how the various different parts of the organization fit together. One also needs some management training because there are management skills: being a manager is not something you can just do. One needs clear thinking and an ability to think up new ideas.

You need to be quite strategic but you can get that understanding in various ways. For example as I did by organizing a theatre team. You also need to be strong because each consultant and each purchaser has his own view of what you should do.

I worry about where we shall get future managers from when managers are getting such a bad press.

HOW HAVE THE CHANGES SINCE 1989 AFFECTED THE JOB?

The job did exist before the changes but as a deputy general manager post. The focus is now on the clinical service that is being delivered. The main change is the uncertainty, so that one cannot really plan more than a year ahead. In 1992/3, one purchaser said he wanted to buy plastic surgery that year. The next year they said it was not a high priority and they did not want it because we had got rid of their waiting lists. Therefore they would buy hip replacements instead. What was I supposed to do with that plastic surgery service, because a year later they wanted it again? That sort of thing causes a bit of insecurity to this job; you have to learn to look into the future as far as you can, to create the stability that I think a leader should be doing.

I do not think there is a mushrooming of managers, we have the same head count as we ever had. What has mushroomed is finance and information: information technology has changed the most. I fight quite strongly on behalf of the clinical specialties; finance and information is an overhead to them. It takes time to get experienced clinical people in place and opening up wards cannot be done overnight. The support staff we have to keep fluid: if fundholding disappears we do not need a finance department chasing fundholding bills.

PRICE OF LEADERSHIP

One of the downsides is that it can seem a fairly thankless task, a bit lonely, nobody seems to care whether I am there or not. It is human nature to want someone to say 'thank you and well done'.

AND REWARDS

The great rewards are being able to have your visions and personal beliefs put into practice.

HOW DO YOU SEE THE FUTURE?

I think I am lucky, because I am directly responsible to the chief executive, so I can get his ear very easily. There is trust because I have worked with him for a long time. I am allowed to take an idea and work through it and to have some corporate roles as well. I chair the implementation of our IT system, which will be very useful for me in the future. I represent the Radcliffe Infirmary on an Oxford/Anglia group looking at the future of fundholding, so I am working at that sort of level from the secure base of the Infirmary.

Most places are now saying, degree or management qualification, so I am taking an MSc in public service management at Southbank. I get a lot of support from David Wilson and the RI, and they accept that I am not there on 30 Tuesdays a year. People get used to it. I go into work on Sundays sometimes and I have had to prioritize. On a normal day I am in at 7.00 am and I leave at 6.00 pm.

My next aim is to be a chief executive of a small unit, or a director of operations of a bigger unit. I have had a lot of acute sector leadership, maybe I ought to be looking elsewhere.

2.   Doctors as managers

It is noteworthy that most of the doctors do not think of themselves as leaders, unlike those interviewed from other career backgrounds.
Two of the doctors are above the target age of 35 or less for young leaders, because the long medical training makes it more likely that they will come to leadership positions later.

Case studies 7 and 8
Two hospital consultants

Case study 7

Peter Worlock, Consultant Trauma and Orthopaedic Surgeon, Chair of the Critical Care Clinical Centre at the Oxford Radcliffe NHS Trust from 1991–95.

Peter Worlock, who is 41, took up the new post of chair of the critical care centre four years ago. He is just giving it up, feeling that he needs time for his private life.

He had no previous training in management, although he did work for a time in North America and Europe where he took an interest in the hospital structures. He also read about the Griffiths proposals when they came out and was involved in the Resource Management Initiative in the Northern RHA. So he had a little relevant background; otherwise he had to learn on the hoof. It was a very steep learning curve to know what people were talking about in management terms and to pick up the necessary financial information. Learning enough accounting was essential for building up business cases.

You had to be seen by colleagues as being credible managerially, but also remaining credible clinically. You had to show that you were able to deliver what you said you would deliver.

WHO HELPED YOU TO LEARN THE CLINICAL MANAGEMENT ROLE?

Tracy Allen, who started as a business manager when I started as service centre chair. She had been an NHS management trainee and was able to teach me about the managerial side while I taught her about the medical perspective. This was the only help that I got and I had no formal training.

WHAT DO YOU SEE LEADERSHIP AS BEING?

You have to be able to supply a clear vision that is acceptable to and understandable by the people with whom you work. You have to be able to motivate people to share that vision. The vision here is to be the best critical care centre in the country and in Europe, where anyone who is injured will receive optimum care.

You have to be able to identify people who are capable of achieving things that they may not realize that they can do, and then motivate them to do so. Then you need to give them the wherewithal in responsibility and power to do it: doing that is difficult because one has to give up something. You need to see them regularly to discuss and review how they are getting on.

People who work in the trenches must know you and see you and know that you are willing to roll up your sleeves and get down to it. You must be credible in the trenches doing the mundane work and doing it well, not just doing the interesting work. I think they must know that you are not asking them to do something because you are shedding it, but because you think they can do it best.

DO YOU THINK OF YOURSELF AS A LEADER?

Not really, I do not think of what I do as leadership but as motivating and energizing people. However, one senior nurse said to me, 'I came in saying I was not going to do something, then I realized you made me think I wanted to do it'. You should try to shape things so that people feel that it is their idea. You are trying to open them up to different ways of doing things, but giving them time to reach their own conclusions. That can be irritating because of the delay, but it works better. You need to talk to people, talk logically, providing the evidence for what you are suggesting. Try to encourage them to come back to you with their own ideas. Although you may need to keep nudging them back along the corridor that you see as possible.

EXAMPLE OF A LEADERSHIP ACTION

We now have round the clock consultant cover so as to provide the best care for patients. This idea became accepted by gradually building up the case for the change. The first task was getting consultant agreement; partly this happened through retirements and getting in new people who were in favour. When we had got to three consultants in favour and two opposed we were able to manage the opposition by saying, 'you can develop your own speciality and we can bring other people for the general consultant cover'. When we had consultant agreement, there was a task of convincing other people, particularly those in finance, that the change would be viable and cost effective. Keith Willett, another consultant trauma surgeon, and I tried to work the new rota as much as we could to build up the case. We were able to show that it was cost effective and that it improved care; for example, that it reduced the number of people coming back to outpatients. Once we were able to show that it was cost effective, a lot of opposition disappeared. Then there was the mechanics of setting it up. Keith did this by setting up small groups of relevant players to work out how it would be done in their own area.

Another aspect of getting the change accepted was recruiting people, new consultants and some new senior nurses who agreed with this way of working.

There was tremendous opposition outside; for example, a senior medical figure said at a large public dinner, six months after we had got it going, that we were 'traitors to the medical profession'. What he was objecting to was 24 hour consultant cover.

DO YOU THINK OF YOURSELF AS A ROLE MODEL?

No, because I do not do things effectively and because I am bad tempered and not a good delegator, so I am not a good example.

WHAT HAVE YOU LEARNT?

That the idea of continual consultant cover 'in house' can be done; also that doctors can function in a managerial role with the appropriate training. You will not do some things as well as the professional managers and finance people, but you can effect change and influence the strategy.

That a managerial role is extraordinarily time consuming on top of clinical work, so there has to be some way of freeing up time. It needs to be done on a half-time basis, because then you can get adequate medical cover and you can also give more to the managerial job. One or two sessions is not adequate because you cannot get adequate locum cover.

I have learnt some skills, finance and accounting, the managerial language and how to talk sensibly with professional managers and to use some of their tools.

That you cannot treat managers like doctors nor doctors like managers, they think in different ways. What you can do is try to give each a perspective on the other.

I have learnt humility, when I realized that I was not doing the job effectively. I thought that I was doing it less well than I did before but others might think differently. I learnt that you cannot do everything.

Luckily I did not have to learn a great deal on the relationship side. Nurses are generally better at relationships than doctors, who are very variable. I have not had difficulties with relationships; I have been relating to patients of very different kinds since I was 20. You need to be able to listen before you start talking.

I had to talk to a consultant colleague about how he was doing his job when he was having difficulty coping. This was very difficult because consultants are not appraised. Perhaps there should be a regular appraisal, then it would be easier because reviewing somebody's work would then be a familiar concept.

That sometimes you have to be second.

STILL NEED TO LEARN?

Yes, one must always be learning. On one time you work out a business case and present it and it goes well; another time it does not and you have to think why is that? I am always having to learn from what does not work

properly, asking: 'what am I doing wrong'? In that sense, I am still learning all the time, though I do not think I need to learn more in finance.

PRICE AND REWARDS

One reward is being able to see that we are providing much better, yet
cheaper care, to patients. Related to that is being able to show people
that you can do it.

Professional recognition is also a reward; we have had twelve trusts
and health authorities visit us to look at what we are doing and some of
them have asked us to help them with it – that is, of course, another
demand on one's time. There are now four trusts in the country where
there is 24-hour consultant cover in either A & E or ITU. There are also
many more where there is a greater acceptance of the need for consultant
involvement.

The major cost is the time that it takes. We did a study of the time that
we spent and found that it was 55 hours a week in direct NHS work – we
do no private work. Then there are seven to ten hours on routine administration of the kind that any consultant would do; added to that is 12 to
15 hours a week for the hospital management role. I had not realized it
was quite so much until we actually checked it. This meant that one was
spending 80 hours a week physically in the hospital; this is just too
much, which is why I have decided to step down. It has meant that I
have virtually no outside activities. For instance, I have not played golf
for four years, nor have I had sufficient time to spend with my wife.

ADVICE TO OTHER CLINICAL MANAGERS

Do not think that becoming a clinical director is a chore; it is immensely
rewarding because you can improve patient care.

It is helpful to have some formal structured training before you take
on the post. It is training that should go on over a period of time.

Try and listen to what the business managers are saying.

Try and learn how the hospital decision structure works; even if you
want to change it you will not be able to do that at the start.

Do not do it for too long, because of the time that it takes.

FUTURE

I might plan to come back to some form of clinical management later. In
the longer term, I would not see myself in full time clinical work but
doing some mix of clinical and managerial work. We are moving to a
project-based system of change, so managing projects is the most likely
thing for me to do here.

Case study 8

Dr Fergus Gleeson, Consultant radiologist and consultant in administrative charge of radiology at the Churchill Hospital, Oxford.

Dr Fergus Gleeson, who is 34, became consultant radiologist at the Churchill Hospital when he was 31. As he was the only radiologist he had to take over the running of the department. He was clinical director until the hospital merged with the John Radcliffe to form the Oxford Radcliffe Trust. Then he became consultant in administrative charge, with the clinical director being at the John Radcliffe. Now the work takes just a few hours a week, but before it took quite a lot longer.

WHAT IS DIFFERENT ABOUT YOUR PRESENT JOB FROM THE PREVIOUS ONE?

The greatest difference from the previous medical posts was having responsibility as a consultant for staff and equipment and for the future of the department. The major change was having an ability to control what is happening although in practice this is less than the theory because there is less flexibility.

Now that I am not the clinical director and have this lesser post, I miss the immediately up-to-date information and having less clout. Because of the latter it is more difficult to decide what is going to happen, for example, on staff gradings; as it is not my decision it just takes longer.

WHAT DO YOU SEE LEADERSHIP AS BEING?

It is the person where the buck stops. The people who are good at it are those who can make decisions without feeling too guilty about their effects; who can get others to agree with the decision even if it is not the one they want.

Leadership is making decisions about direction and coordinating people. Outsiders may think that a hospital consists of a lot of people all doing the same thing, but that is not so, there is such a lot of conflict. Even in a small radiology department with people wanting different kinds of equipment.

DO YOU THINK OF YOURSELF AS A LEADER?

No, rather as a teacher. Many consultants may see themselves as leaders but most of them are not. Leadership is a team game and doctors are not trained for that.

Consultants have a small team which they organize well, but they find it much harder to translate this into leading in a larger group. Most doctors do not do that very well.

HOW DO YOU TRY TO LEAD?

Fergus, though disclaiming being a leader, was happy to answer how he tried to carry out a leadership role.

I try to inform people about what is happening, how it is going to happen and why, and why what they want to happen is or is not possible. I do it by discussion, I also try to lead by example, by being seen to be reasonable and by working hard. People need to understand that what you are doing, although it may not be what they want, is reasonable. You just have to make a decision to the best of your ability, try to convince other people that it is reasonable and stick with it.

WHAT ARE THE MAIN OPPORTUNITIES FOR LEADERSHIP IN YOUR JOB?

Problem solving; when people bring problems to me, I have to solve them. Another aspect is trying to work out where the department is going. I must be concerned with those forward-looking decisions.

DO YOU THINK OF YOURSELF AS A ROLE MODEL?

Not in the sense of implying that I am doing things right. Trying to get junior doctors to recognize that reaching treatment decisions requires a lot of facts.

LEADERSHIP ACTIVITIES OUTSIDE WORK

None, apart from my family and a bit of social sport; I do not know how some people find time for other things.

WHAT DO YOU FEEL THAT YOU HAVE LEARNED?

Once you get involved in management you realize that as a doctor there are many things happening that you did not know about. Unless you are involved in management you do not realize how complex things are, nor the consequences of making changes.

STILL NEED TO LEARN?

To get better at making the right decisions and communicating to colleagues and staff. I think with experience you make decisions more easily; anything you do repeatedly gets easier, so does staff management. It is not too hard to learn the factual basis like accountancy.

PRICE OF LEADERSHIP

The price is the stress and the worries that go with being clinical director, and the personal time that it takes, though these costs are less in my current role. Another price is that people blame you for what you cannot change.

AND THE REWARDS

One of the rewards is that you learn how you can change things.

WHAT/WHO HELPED YOU GET WHERE YOU ARE?

Lots of very nice helpful consultants, and the fact that my father is vice-dean of Westminster Medical School and a consultant also helped.

ADVICE TO SOMEONE ASPIRING TO BE A CLINICAL DIRECTOR

When you are a new consultant it is better to concentrate on the medical side and only come to management later. I did not have this option; it is a bit much to expect people to do both. I think I would have done it better if I had come to it later, although I do not regret it.

You need to be well briefed for the role; go on a management course where they explain the terminology so that you are comfortable with it when it is used in management meetings.

OTHER POINTS

The difference for managers in the NHS compared to say the army is that they do not understand the technical side of it.

Nurses are better at developing management skills than doctors.

Most doctors get bored with what they are doing after about 20 years and may then want to take up management. I like medicine and do not particularly like the managerial responsibility for other people's lives.

Case studies 9 and 10
Two GPs

Case study 9

Dr Paul Roblin, GP, Banbury Road, Summertown, Oxford.

Paul Roblin is 41, and one of 8 partners in the practice. Currently it is not a fundholding practice but will be going into community fundholding.

He is the executive partner; this post is elected annually, but he has done it for the last ten years. He is a member of the local medical committee (LMC) and of its executive board. He is also one of four representatives from LMC who negotiate with the FHSA. He is the GP lead for the health authority in negotiations with the major Oxford trust, the Oxford Radcliffe. He is also on other committees on an *ad hoc* basis. Altogether these take five to ten per cent of his time.

WHAT IS DIFFERENT ABOUT THESE ACTIVITIES FROM THAT OF A GP?

As a GP one is concerned with individuals. In my other roles I am concerned with strategy and thinking in population terms. I am also more concerned with costs/benefit analysis.

DO YOU SEE YOURSELF AS A LEADER?

In my external role, it is more as a representative. It is very much leadership with a small 'l' because I am a representative.

As an executive partner in the practice I may make decisions, but they must be ratified in practice meetings. In my meetings outside I am very much a representative. General practice is a non-hierarchical structure; you try to achieve consensus in the practice as a whole. If this is not achieved, it is the doctors who decide because they have a greater financial stake and because they stay longer; in addition there is the traditional role of doctors.

HOW DO YOU TRY TO LEAD?

By achieving consensus, by the use of knowledge, discussion, pragmatism and logic, by listening and by communicating well.

I am wary of leaders who promote their own views, rather than act as a representative. I would find it difficult to promote something that is a minority view. One has to restrain the impulse to promote one's own view.

There is a problem in a large partnership where we work by consensus, because this in effect gives one person the right of veto.

I believe in dealing with things as they come up; important with paperwork to bin it or deal with it.

MAIN OPPORTUNITIES FOR LEADERSHIP IN YOUR JOB?

By anticipating issues, proposing solutions, responding to feedback, showing assertiveness on the basis of my electorate in dealing with outside bodies.

EXAMPLES OF LEADERSHIP ACTIONS

Most difficult was when the four of us who negotiate with the FHSA agreed the way in which the GMS (General Medical Services) money would be rationed by differential cuts. This decision was opposed by very vocal self-interest groups, so we had to stand firm. Another example is having to advise on the nature of rationing because this is an area where doctors feel uncomfortable.

DO YOU SEE YOURSELF AS A ROLE MODEL?

Yes, I am very aware of the image that one presents and how that can give you credibility. You have your own concept of what is a desirable image, in the hope that other people will see it as admirable. I strive quite hard to present a good image so that people respect what I do. I want to be respected rather than loved, and this dictates my behaviour: respected by being consistent and assertive.

LEADERSHIP ACTIVITIES OUTSIDE WORK?

Very little time, my outside activities are not ones that require leadership.

WHAT HAVE YOU LEARNED AS A LEADER?

Tactics within a committee, the use of image, to become a better compromiser and to be more pragmatic, also that one cannot change everything.

STILL NEED TO LEARN?

One is constantly learning by doing and reflecting on one's experience.

EFFECTS OF THE NHS CHANGES FROM 1989 ON?

One's work has been dominated by the changes, as GP opinion is now increasingly sought.

ADVICE TO OTHERS?

Only get involved in management and representation if it really interests you. Be prepared to work hard to gain the necessary knowledge to be able to contribute to decisions and to have an influence. Learn to be confident in committees and to articulate well; be assertive. You need a fine balance between being thick skinned, to cope with the stress from criticism and with making mistakes and yet sensitive to the views of one's constituents and co-committee members and ready to modify one's own views.

PRICE OF LEADERSHIP

The down side is that it is exhausting at times. If you are not sufficiently thick skinned, the political role and the difficulties in it can get to you. I believe in a multifactorial life so that one can balance different aspects of it.

AND ITS REWARDS

It is exhilarating to be involved in medicine in different ways; then there is the social element as one gets an enhanced social network. There is also a financial reward for the time one spends. One gains self esteem when things go well. The variety of the types of work keeps you stimulated and there is a cross-over, the knowledge you gain is also useful in patient care.

Case study 10

Dr Tim Wilson, GP, The Mill Stream Surgery, Benson, Oxford.

Tim Wilson is 33, he has worked for the last five years in a two-partner practice, which has a practice manager, assistant doctor and a trainee. It is a joint fundholding practice with a neighbouring practice. He is joint lead partner for fundholding which is run in the Mill Stream surgery. His outside medical activities include being locality forum chair, a member of the local medical committee, the medical audit committee, GP advisory committee to the health authority, chair of a local GP computer group and a member of the prescribing purchasing committee.

There are 20 people in the surgery, eight of whom are employed, the others are attached staff.

WHAT IS DIFFERENT ABOUT THE MANAGERIAL SIDE OF YOUR WORK NOW COMPARED WITH PREVIOUS JOBS?

It is totally different to previous jobs. As an undergraduate you have no managerial training and when I was a GP trainee there was little or none. It is something which you have never done before and which brings different skills and a different way of thinking.

The relationship with people is different as a partner; you become responsible for the running of the practice and the care of your patients. Your relationship with patients changes because of increasing managerial skills and with the responsibility. Before being a partner you are one who is managed; as a partner you become a manager with responsibilities.

WHAT DO YOU SEE LEADERSHIP AS BEING?

Leading people by example and motivating people. Leadership requires encouragement and direction of others in the broadest sense.

In this surgery we went through the process of making a mission statement and manifesto. This is something I am proud of and was a great step forward in leading the surgery.

DO YOU THINK OF YOURSELF AS A LEADER?

Yes I do, I have to be in a small practice. In a small practice it is impossible to shrink into the background, and there is the ability to change things quickly.

EXAMPLES OF WHERE LEADERSHIP IS REQUIRED?

Reception staff have an impossible job; it is vital that the partners give a clear message to them so that they are able to deal with patients in a consistent manner, knowing when to be firm and when to relent to requests.

The development of clinical work including audit and protocol requires leadership.

The development of a five year plan for the practice.

The development of a practice 'ethos'.

DO YOU SEE YOURSELF AS A ROLE MODEL?

Not consciously, but I must be in the example of how I deal with patients for staff to follow. In a small community where the doctor is well known their lifestyle is a role model of sorts.

ANY LEADERSHIP ACTIVITIES OUTSIDE WORK?

I am a school governor.

WHAT HAVE YOU LEARNT AS A LEADER?

You learn to manage yourself, I have a much more focused idea of what I want to do.

As a team member your role as a leader changes your relationship with others. There will have to be difficult and perhaps unpopular decisions.

One also makes mistakes which, for a while, cause a bad atmosphere. For instance, we identified some small problems in reception, minor niggles. At the same time we were keen to see how we could improve their training to enable them to share their skills; we identified using a video as a method. Unfortunately, it was seen that a video was a way of policing these problems; not the idea at all. We have now used role play as a means of training, quite successfully.

STILL NEED TO LEARN?

Yes, but I am not sure what. There is no structure within general practice to identify learning needs in respect of management although there are more and more courses in this field.

USEFUL FORMS OF LEARNING?

Modular courses; I was lucky enough to join the Oxford Region higher training course which has stood me in good stead for management training.

Since we have become fundholders I have had 'business' type training which has helped our management skills.

My partner is a better manager than most GPs and I have learnt from him.

I belong to a young practitioners' group (as part of the modular course mentioned above); this helps us all deal with difficult leadership issues by sharing.

ADVICE TO OTHERS

Avoid isolation. I know of young GPs who did not have the contact of their contemporaries and they have now left general practice.

Involve yourself in things outside general practice, otherwise you can quickly become stale.

REWARDS AND PRICE

There is satisfaction when things go well, such as our practice manifesto; it was a team effort and came from the heart. There is reward when patients praise you; we recently had a battle with a chemist, the patients came out on our side and supported us in a very pleasing way (2000 patients wrote in support of us).

GPs are not valued for the leadership they do, especially in terms of remuneration. GP fundholders are paid a pittance for the managerial work they do.

There is a price in the extra pressures it puts on you juggling leadership tasks and clinical work. This could lead to extra pressures at home which can only be avoided if protected.

FUTURE

I shall stay as a GP. In the next two years I would like to involve myself in research, particularly the way receptionists work and are trained; their job is an impossible one, unable to please patient and doctor at the same time.

Using the case studies

The following questions can help you to consider the lessons that you could draw from the case studies in this chapter.

GENERALLY

1. What do the case studies tell you about the implications for a clinician of taking on a managerial role?
2. What conclusions do you draw about the effects of the organizational changes on doctors' and nurses' careers?
3. What struck you most about what was said? What lessons should you draw?
4. What similarities do you see with the lessons from the case studies in Chapter 10? Are there any significant differences?

FOR NURSES

From the Case Studies of the Two Nurses

1. What lessons should you draw from the two nurses' careers? Which route appeals more to you? Why?
2. What lessons should you draw about effective leadership?
3. Where do you think each of them should seek to go next in their careers? Why?
4. Do you agree with the importance of being a role model?
5. What is the most useful advice that they give?

From the Two Part Case Study 5a and 5b

1. Comparing the two cases; in what ways are they similar? in what ways are they different? Why?
2. Which of the two jobs would you find most satisfying? Why?
3. What do you think her staff will remember her for when she leaves?
4. Would you like to work for her? Why? or Why not?

The twin aspects of leadership

Case study 11

A DGM

The aims of this case study are to illustrate two key aspects of leadership and many of the subjects discussed earlier. It is retained in a shortened form in this new edition because, despite the changes in the NHS, it still illustrates many aspects of leadership, and the research on which it is based enabled a much fuller picture to be given of how the individual leads, than is possible in the single interviews on which the other case studies are based.

Case Study 11 focuses on how this DGM saw his leadership role and how others saw him, rather than on the goals that he was seeking to achieve. It is an in-depth study deriving from the Templeton tracer study of district general managers, see Appendix A. Peter Lawrence (a pseudonym) was a member of that study. Frequent discussions were held with him over two years and four months and he supplied a weekly record of his activities and contacts over two years. All his principal contacts were interviewed, some of them more than once. Their comments about him form part of this case.

Background information

THE DISTRICT

It is a medium sized district in an expanding area. There is a concentration of services on one site on the edge of a town, and one other main area of services in another part of the district. All the main health services are provided and there is a new district general hospital. The district is fortunate in its land assets.

THE DGM

He is in his late 40s and has spent his working life in health service management. He was previously the district administrator in the same district, which post he had held since the late 1970s. Before then the district had been known for its staff problems. When Peter became DGM the district was operating successfully.

Guidelines for action in the early days

All the DGMs in the tracer study were asked about these. Peter was one of the few who found it easy to answer. These were his guides in the early days of the Griffiths reorganization:

1. In carrying out the reorganization, to be radical in a conservative guise by retaining titles but changing content.
2. To build on the good relationships that he had established as district administrator.
3. Concern for individuals so that in the reorganization jobs were matched to people and no-one was jettisoned; to use existing managers but to change their approach to management. Only one new person was brought in and that only when the chief nursing officer decided to take early retirement.
4. To pick up the Griffiths ideas and sell them hard, explaining why with general management there had to be changes; particularly continuing the process of devolution started earlier.
5. To set objectives and measure progress against them. He attached great importance to this, so that a regular process of reviewing his subordinates against objectives was instituted from the early days.
6. The importance of publicizing to the community what the district is doing, producing an annual report for this purpose, and of making the organization sensitive and receptive to the public's opinions.
7. Advising DHA members about objectives and target dates so that they knew what to expect, and how to assess progress.

He described his task in the early days as follows:

> I've got to use one cohort of existing managers to help me change others because I can't relate to everybody myself...it's a bit like the New Testament, I am trying to convert my disciples to my aims and then I've got to send them out to preach to the rest, and changing them round is quite difficult – that is the biggest constraint.

He also spoke of one of the most difficult and necessary tasks for a leader in a time of change – and that is when leadership is most necessary:

> To keep on an even keel in times of change and to present to the district health authority and to the outside world a confident and stable facade.

What others expected of the DGM

The most common expectations were:

1. *Support,* particularly when times are difficult, 'so that I know that I can go ahead with what we have agreed with the confidence of his support'.
2. *Clear indication of priorities* for my work and of how he sees the district going.
3. *Minimum interference* 'that he trusts me to get on with the job without leaning over my shoulder'.

A variety of other expectation were mentioned by senior staff, thinking about their relationship with him, including:

- positive leadership;
- to be honest with me, but tactful;
- regular contact and to be available when help is needed;
- never to get angry;
- to treat me with respect;
- professional guidance, and expertise in areas where I am ignorant;
- that his expectations of me will be reasonable.

In the main, those interviewed said that Peter met their expectations.

The chair and vice-chair had different kinds of expectations, which Peter also met:

> To be right in there at the patient interface. To be much more involved than as district administrator in ensuring that clinical practice was the most efficient we could attain, and in questioning clinicians on why they do what they do and on how they organize things.

> That the buck should stop with him.

Peter's views on leadership

WHAT IS LEADERSHIP?

Leadership is being high profile: shaping the choices and the priorities. Putting the decisions up in a way that cannot be avoided, and yet recognizing that there are times when you have to bow to the inevitable and will not get what you want.

It is being confident in yourself and in your own evaluation and decision-making process.

There are two halves to it: expressing yourself, showing the district what you are and where you are going; and relating to those people who want to follow you.

Leadership is very personal. It is partially to do with status in the organization, but it is much more than that. It is almost charismatic. It is you using yourself and your attributes and quite consciously sometimes.

There are all sorts of roles in which you have to be the leader. Outside the district as representative spokesman, willy nilly you have become a public figure and are asked to speak on all sorts of occasions.

THE TWO HALVES OF LEADERSHIP

I am quite fascinated by military views; if you read Mountbatten, Montgomery or Wellington, all tremendous leaders, they have the same two qualities. First, they are quite sure where they are going, and they mostly have the political skill to sell it. Second, they relate to the troops at any and every level on a personal basis. What they are doing, what you are doing, is saying: 'Yes, I am the leader, but all the time I am recognizing you for your worth and what you are'. It is what I am very conscious of doing when I chair the joint consultative committee.

1. *Expressing yourself* – My sort of leadership is to do with me. Usually I would see it as me at the apex of the arrow, pushing at the centre. So you have to know what you are about. You have to be reasonably clear on your own directions.
2. *Relating to others* – You must recognize them as individuals; afford them room to grow and to express disagreement. You should get on to a basis where they acknowledge your leadership without feeling dominated by it.

In leadership in relation to the health authority and to the consultants I apply the same principles, but in a slightly more subtle way because there is no line relationship. With both these groups it is very important that you know what your goals are and that, generally speaking, it is clear to them what you are about. In seeking to get the health authority members to follow my lead, and in trying to encourage the consultants in the same way, I am trying to establish a personal relationship with each of them.

I pay a lot of attention to what the members want. If they ever ask me for anything, I go to some trouble to respond. I am saying to them very strongly: 'I see you as an individual and I want to listen to what you have got to say and to recognize your concerns'. That does not inhibit me from disagreeing with them, particularly in the formal situation, and relying on the strength of the relationship to carry you through a difficult period.

The same principles apply with my general mangers. I am sometimes asked whether I have disagreements with them. Of course, I have quite sharp disagreements. There are occasions when you know there is an issue that you cannot afford to lose, so you want to dominate and to win it. But you hope that the strength of the relationship, its personal nature and the feel of the target that you are after, will carry you through such disagreements.

I could reckon to carry that through with the general managers and with the members, but I could not always do that with the consultant body. There will be times when they reject me and my leadership, then I have to fall back on other devices to get what I want.

Then there are the public occasions like a retirement party, when I am adopting the same approach to leadership. I am talking both to the person retiring and to the others, spreading some messages, increasing the understanding between all of us. I think of Mountbatten going round the South-east Asian Command and jumping on top of the Land Rover and having that ability to communicate to up to 500 and get it across.

OTHER ASPECTS OF LEADERSHIP

3. *Sharing leadership* – Another interesting aspect of leadership – and I am not quite sure that I fully understand it – is that most of the time you need to be clear and confident, but there are occasions when you need not be. There are times when you can step back a bit from the role and let other people share in it.

4. *Bow down occasionally* – One special characteristic of leadership in the NHS is that though you are the leader, the head of the arrow, you have to accept that there are times when you are going to be humbled, not humiliated, but humbled. You cannot win everything and to do so would be bad policy. Sometimes you just have to recognize you will be defeated and be sensible and live with that; sometimes you can arrange little defeats or concessions. People like a leader; they like the strength and the reliability of somebody who

knows his own mind. At the same time they will resent somebody who is infallible, or somebody who thinks he is. So, as well as drawing back to let other people share the leadership, you should accept defeats, and accept them ruefully, acknowledging: 'well, I lost that one'.

That is important with the chair. There are some situations which I can concede to him, and one or two where he has been right and I have been wrong, but there are many others where I will step back and say: 'you are probably right there' or go back and say: 'I have thought about it and yes, that is the best way of doing it'. So you are bowing down a bit. And occasionally, of course, with your own subordinates too.

5. *The team* – recollecting what I have said, I have not used the word 'team' once. Leadership is not without other individuals, but leadership is one individual. Others will contribute but a team does not lead. The team is there, but they are very much my team – how possessive I feel about my managers!
    [*This view contrasts with the discussion in Chapter 6 on team working; the contrast suggests the change that has been taking place towards a more participative approach.*]
6. *Dangers of leadership* – Megalomania is quite a danger. If you are a leader as I have been describing it, then your big stumbling block is that you start to think that you are always right. That is encouraged because you get lots of toadies creeping round you because you are the boss, and you have to distinguish them from those who quite genuinely have something different to say that you ought to listen to.

You need a recognition of people's legitimate points of view. Listening to other people's criticisms is very important. It is not always easy, but if you are patient about it you can let other people's contribution influence the way you shape things. I am sometimes irritated by the advice that I get because it will slow down what I want to get done, but I have to recognize that I need to listen.

There is a balance needed: if you listen too much you get paralysed. You start to worry about your own values. If you lose self-confidence you are a dead duck, but if you allow self-confidence to become megalomania then you are also a dead duck.

How he leads, as seen by his main contacts

By being a very distinctive personality:

His personal strengths are that he is educated, has a sharp intelligence, a strong individual personality, a unique identity as a person, a very strong sense of humour, a positive leader with a lot of charisma.

By being passionately, emotionally, committed to the NHS:

He believes in the business that we are in... sometimes some of us get involved in the technicalities and he's likely to say: 'come on there's a group of people out there, that's what it is about'.

He has the patient in mind all the time and everything that he does is related to that; he wants everybody else to be better motivated to accomplish that idea and is upset if they are not.

One of his greatest strengths was seen to be his capacity to relate to other people:

In those instances of excellent management that I have met, every employee feels that the manager has his eye on them. And however many levels there are between them and the manager at the top, they leapfrog those and relate psychologically to the man at the top. I think Peter has that ability.

Comparing him with other managers in the region, he's by far the most outgoing. So it makes it fairly easy to get rapport and, of course, there are the ties. It's part of the image. It's helpful because we are trying to change the image of the organization and anything that projects humanity rather than process is helpful...It is the willingness to make oneself personally identifiable.

One of Peter's distinctive methods of managing is his friendliness and his ability to know the names even of the most junior members of staff.

He know what is going on:

He works in an informal roving way. I have to be well-informed of what is happening in my unit otherwise he finds out before I do.

Another strength is his persuasive ability:

He's a superb persuader.

His very skilled way of presenting demands, setting out his instructions very clearly and explaining the context.

He is decisive and supportive:

> If you go to him for advice he will quickly decide, and if you have a problem he won't fob you off. I feel part of a team. I like, too, that if he has confidence in you he delegates to you and does not look over your shoulder. But I also feel that he is available when I need him.

His trustworthiness is important:

> He has a lot of integrity, I trust him... I know if it gets rough he will support me, he won't back off at the last moment and leave me exposed.

He provides stimulus:

> There's a lot going on, it's a lively place. He's very innovative; he stimulates people; he's very supportive; he's very flexible. You can get an answer quickly and he'll let you do something different... It's very rarely that you get something back with a 'no', that's why I say he's easy to work for. Very receptive to ideas and to using people in different ways.

His intellectual abilities are admired:

> He's got an enormous capacity to keep close to a fair amount of detail across a very, very wide range, paradoxically he's also extremely good at seeing the wood for the trees.

> His superb speech, his accurate use of words, and he can be moving on occasions at a farewell do.

Two criticisms made of his leadership were that he can expect too much and criticize too readily:

> There is a world of difference if somebody says to me 'I am disappointed but I realise you are trying very hard' or 'I am disappointed why don't you try harder'.

And that he sometimes criticized someone in front of others.

Leading in different relationships

This section describes Peter's aims and actions in dealing with the relationships in the different aspects of his job.

RELATIONSHIPS WITH THE CHAIR

Peter had the same chair throughout the study period. Both he and the chair saw their relationship as a very important one.

Peter thinks that it is essential to make sure of having the chair's support, particularly on contentious issues.

His actions helped to shape his chair's role. He thought a lot about how to make the relationship an effective one, as he did about all his major relationships. Even so, in the final interview he said:

> I think I have probably undervalued him for a long time, I am beginning to see his value and his strengths and perhaps if I had been a bit quicker about seeing how he and I fitted together in management terms, I would have been able to make more use of the balance that we have.

(In the tracer study we noticed that many of the DGMs tended to undervalue their chair).

Over the period Peter and his chair learnt to work even better together, as the latter said:

> We have learnt to be frank with each other without taking offence.

An observer at a meeting said to the chair afterwards:

> it is remarkable how well you and the DGM gell, so that you each come in as appropriate.

RELATIONSHIPS WITH THE DISTRICT HEALTH AUTHORITY

Peter sees the members' role being to challenge policy put to them. He said that he wanted to make them feel that they can make a positive impact without raising their expectations too much about what they can do. He ran a one day seminar to help them to explore what role they should play.

The vice-chair described Peter as being always helpful and available to members, and having, via his director of education, launched a programme to help members with their role on mental health appeals and disciplinary appeals. He also said:

> Peter is good in being quite willing and capable of defending his officers against members when they criticize unfairly.

RELATIONSHIP WITH CHC

The CHC (Community Health Council) secretary said:

> His approach has not changed over time. When he first arrived he said to me: 'we are going to have some unpalatable things to say to each other, so let's establish a good working relationship'.

> CHC members appreciate Peter because he does take the trouble to explain the decisions as do the other officers. They appreciate, too, the fact that he considers the CHC to be important and will listen to what they say. When they ask for something it's dealt with whether it is trivial or important.

Peter has seen the CHC as part of the consumer network to which he attaches considerable importance. One of his aims is to empower the customer.

RELATIONSHIP WITH IMMEDIATE STAFF

Peter uses a variety of different ways of communicating with staff reporting to him; he sees each of them regularly on their own for an hour to an hour and a half, about once a fortnight or once a month. These meetings start by the manager briefing him on what is going on and raising anything that he or she wants to. Then Peter 'chases me on any issues that he's concerned about and raises general issues'. There are also informal contacts when needed, but these are infrequent. He is actively involved in guiding, monitoring and encouraging the work of all the managers, taking a particularly active interest in planning, and improving quality and the standard of nursing education.

He coordinates by means of informal meetings in his office. If there are any problems between individual managers he will try to sort it out informally.

RELATIONS WITH CONSULTANTS

Peter was one of the most active of the tracer DGMs in seeking to involve consultants in management, in tackling any consultant who he judged not to be fulfilling his contract, and in trying to ensure that behaviour that was detrimental for patients was tackled by the representative consultants. He saw his role as general manager as having given him more power than he had before to influence consultants' behaviour.

He spent more time with consultants than most of the other DGMs in the tracer study. He sought to involve them in management in a wide variety of ways: clinical budgeting, persuading a consultant to chair a working party on information, and having regular meetings with consultants in lead positions such as the chair of the medical executive committee. [*He was ahead of his time; since then the changes introduced from 1989 have meant that consultants are more actively involved in management.*]

He worked with the relevant consultants, together with the unit general manager concerned, on changes to improve particular services; for example, one of the consultants, who though critical of general management, said:

> A lot of good work has been done on orthopaedics. That's a very solid achievement, an achievement of general management: an achievement because of the amount of political will tackling an issue that had been going on a long time.

One comment about his personal approach to consultants was:

> I think he acts as a focus for the consultants' anxieties. They will ring him up at a moment's notice and he is very good about seeing them. I believe they rely on him much more than they would admit as an outlet for their anxieties.

[*If such a comment was made now it would be about the trust chief executive.*]

REGIONAL MANAGERS

Peter has strong views about the role of region in relation to districts and became the self-appointed spokesman for district general managers in his region. He has been active in trying to improve the regional review of the district and has got agreement to joint meetings beforehand to ensure thorough preparation. He feels that he has made the district review a positive one, which is beneficial to the district while satisfying the region.

SOCIAL SERVICES

One of Peter's various external activities was seeking to develop more satisfactory arrangements in his county for joint planning. In this he was successful. His chair commented:

> He chairs the joint planning team and has good relationships. It was quite a struggle but now everybody's pleased with it.

OTHER DISTRICT STAFF

The arts coordinator and the chaplain were two unexpected recurrent entries in Peter's diary record. Both illustrate the importance that he attached to the ambience within which patients are treated and staff work.

The job of the arts coordinator is to make environmental improvements inside and outside the group of hospitals on the main site. Currently she has a dozen projects for which she has to raise outside finance. She says:

I tell him what I am doing. He is very well-informed and passionately interested.

Peter and the chaplain meet once a quarter to review what the chaplain has learnt in the district. He thus provides Peter with another source of information about attitudes in the district and Peter feels he gains by sharing some current issues with him. The chaplain says that:

Peter is always very supportive, particularly about training, and always positive about exploring ideas.

Lessons for others as described by his senior staff

We asked those interviewed what lessons they thought Peter's approach to the job had for others. The main points made are given below:

- his accessibility and approachability;
- getting around and meeting people at all levels;
- being easily identifiable
- his willingness to take risks: 'who dares, wins';
- allowing himself to be personally vulnerable;
- trusting his subordinates;
- trying to involve the CHC and the JCC very closely;
- using people creatively when a task appears.

What Peter has learnt

DESCRIBED BY OTHERS

To be a forceful manager and not to tolerate inefficiency in others.

He has changed and is still changing. He is becoming less isolationist, much more thoughtful about the repercussions of what he does outside.

To be more tolerant and patient.

He worries less and achieves more.

He manages his work so that he can get through a great pile without worrying that it will overflow.

DESCRIBED BY HIMSELF

I have learnt a lot about the health service in the context of the wider world...I have been surprised, I think, at the amount that I have learnt.

I have learnt a lot about how doctors behave and why they behave as they do. I feel I have had to learn to understand why it is so difficult.

I have learnt a lot more how to use, in a positive sense, my power within and outside the organization, how to use one's position as 'the boss' to change things.

and more personally, a lot about myself and the enormous pressures and stress of the job.

He commented in the final interview:

The job is also a lot of fun; the trouble is when we have these discussions it always comes out sounding very serious and intense, but there is a lot of fun... and there is the power, the creative side of getting the organization to address issues of what you can do for individuals, patients and staff, in the way you can put issues on the agenda and really get them debated, get them taken seriously, get them changed; that, if anything, has been a wider influence and a wider amount of power than I thought at the start.

Making use of this case study

Ask yourself the following questions or use them as the basis for a group discussion of the case study:

1. What do you think is most distinctive about Peter as a leader? What else is distinctive?

2. What do you agree with in Peter's approach to leadership?
3. Are there any lessons for you? If yes, what? What are you going to do about it/them?
4. Is there anything you disagree with, or have reservations about? If yes, what and why?

More generally:

5. What are the main lessons about leadership in this case study?

PART IV

BECOMING A MORE EFFECTIVE LEADER

Part I described leadership.
Part II sought to help you to lead more effectively in different kinds of relationships.
Part III illustrated leadership in action.

In Part IV it is time for you to think about yourself. You will be a more effective leader if you understand, manage and develop yourself well. These two chapters seek to help you to do so.

CHAPTER 13

Managing the job and yourself

'The management of self is critical. Without it, leaders may do more harm than good.'

(Bennis and Nanus)[1]

Two essential aspects of being an effective leader are first, understanding and managing yourself and second, understanding and managing your job. This chapter draws on what others have learnt to help you to do both better.

The ideal

UNDERSTANDING AND MANAGING YOURSELF

1. You develop **appropriate self-confidence in your ability to cope** and have a realistic recognition of when you need help or should try to get somebody else to lead. It is better to err in being somewhat too confident, rather than too doubtful of your abilities.
2. You **understand your strengths and weaknesses** in knowledge, understanding and skill.
3. You **know how wide or narrow is your understanding of other people**, and other professional groups, so that you can tell when you can trust your own judgement of others.
4. You **understand how you work**: what aspects of a job you tend to concentrate upon and what you are likely to neglect or give too little attention to.
5. You can **recognize your own stress symptoms** and have the sense to take them seriously and to do something about them.
6. You are **aware of what you still need to learn**. The leaders in the case studies had different views on their learning needs which can be used as a guide to thinking about your own learning needs.

UNDERSTANDING THE JOB

1. You have a **realistic view of the scope of the job,** recognize its potential and the factors that constrain you.
2. You can **assess what is good** within your area of responsibility and **needs maintaining** and **what needs changing.**
3. You can **assess** the nature and amount of the **resources available** to you.
4. You have **identified the key relationships.**

AND BEING EFFECTIVE IN IT

1. You **know what you are trying to achieve.** You are alert to potential threats to what you are doing, and want to do, and active in trying to forestall them. You notice and use opportunities that arise to further your aims.
2. You are able to **prioritize your work** and, unless there is good reason not to, to keep to your priorities.
3. You have the self-discipline to **tackle difficult decisions** and never allow things to be fudged – unless by conscious decision.
4. You can both take a **broad view** of the factors relevant to a particular problem and, **when necessary, understand the details.**
5. You can **prevent yourself getting too immersed in operational detail and too attracted by firefighting.**
6. You are aware of the danger of spending **too much time working in areas that you enjoy,** particularly those that really belong to an earlier job – your play area(s) – and exercise the necessary self-discipline.
7. You seek to increase your **understanding** of all **those whose cooperation you need.**
8. You can **manage your time efficiently.** It is an essential ability in very busy jobs, but it is not the most important aspect of managing yourself.

There are, of course, many other factors that are relevant to effectiveness. Some of these are aspects of leadership discussed earlier in this book. The ones described above are aspects of managing your job that you could reasonably set yourself as ideals, because they should be attainable by people with very different personalities.

Difficulties in achieving the ideal

The main difficulties in managing yourself come, not suprisingly, from yourself, but there may also be difficulties inherent in the job and the particular situation within which you work.

DIFFICULTIES FROM YOURSELF

1. **Inadequate self-discipline**. Some people learn early in life the self-discipline that is needed to be an effective leader; others have to painfully acquire it.
2. **Poor organization**. Some people are well organized, others have a struggle to learn to keep on top of the varied demands of their job.
3. **Trapped in operational details**. A common difficulty in more senior jobs is a continuing attraction to operational details and the enjoyment of firefighting.
4. **Inadequate objectivity**. Some people have a greater capacity for objectivity than others. Leaders need to combine commitment, preferably passionate commitment, to the ideal, to the vision of how the organization for which they are responsible should change, with a capacity for detached analysis of the situation. This is a hard combination, but the first is more important than the second and the second is easier to learn.
5. **Too little energy and drive**. The levels of energy and drive as well as ambition differ between individuals, but if you are, or are aspiring to be, a leader you will need to be well above average on all three, though ambition need not be personal – it can be ambition for the achievements of your group.
6. **Self-importance**. Too great an opinion of the importance of your own contribution compared with that of others makes it hard for you to manage, as that is likely to mean that you do too much and delegate too little. Too much misplaced confidence in your managerial abilities is also dangerous – doctors may be more likely than those from other backgrounds to overrate their knowledge and skill in managing.
7. **Inadequate self-confidence**. Conversely too little confidence will make it hard for you to be accepted as a leader.

DIFFICULTIES IN THE JOB AND ITS SITUATION

Some jobs require greater abilities for self-management than others. A barrage of difficult and demanding problems makes it hard to organize your time and to give attention to other important but less immediately pressing problems. Many senior executives in the NHS are finding that it is difficult to cope with the volume of work: the amount of paper to be read and processed, the number of people to be seen and the variety of problems to be tackled. So it is hard to manage oneself in the tough and demanding jobs that accompany major change. A subject mentioned by most of the leaders interviewed for Part III.

Some jobs are inherently more stressful than others, though the sources of stress vary. Inadequate support at work and at home make a great difference to the ease with which you can cope.

One or more of the key relationships may be specially difficult. In many jobs the character of your boss makes a considerable difference to the ease with which you can manage yourself. This is particularly true for a chief executive's relationship with the chair.

So, there are real difficulties in the situation, but however difficult it is you can help yourself.

Steps towards the ideal

UNDERSTANDING AND MANAGING YOURSELF

1. **Developing self-confidence**. The importance of self-confidence, and of appearing confident, is discussed by many of the young leaders in Part III. The tracer DGMs in their final interview often talked about how they had developed self-confidence and how much easier this made it for them.

   A problem for many who get to the top of their particular part of the organization is being **alone up front**, as one chief executive said:

   > At work I have never been anything other than a team member before. I have had to relearn the sort of confidence that I used to have at school when I was captain of sports teams and so on. It's relearning the confidence to be on one's own.

   Self-confidence about your ability to do your job should come with more experience of working in it. It is the more general self-confidence that many younger leaders need to develop. Seeking opportunities for public speaking, even taking a course on public speaking, is a way of gaining confidence on your feet. Taking leadership positions in outside organizations, whether professional bodies, voluntary organizations or sports is another way of developing your confidence and widening your experience of human nature.

   The experienced leader in a challenging job may have to use other means of developing or at least sustaining confidence. A counsellor, confidante or guru, whichever is your inclination and you can find, is someone that most leaders need and with whom they can share and examine their doubts. The burden of appearing confident when you are not may otherwise be too heavy.

2. **Avoiding over-confidence**. The section headed 'megalomania' in the account of Peter in the last case study is a good warning of this danger. You need to have, and to retain, a capacity to listen to critical comments.

3. **Understanding and managing your stress**. This is one of the most essential abilities for any leader in a difficult and demanding job. The first step is recognizing when you are getting too stressed, because the common and dangerous pattern is to deny the stress or to work even harder because you feel you are not coping. A symptom of stress is the belief that you are indispensable!

Individuals have their own stress symptoms: the more common ones are sleeping badly, indigestion and, more for women, tearfulness. Learn to recognize your own and to take heed. Learn, too, what stresses you and try to avoid it if you can or else try to take some recuperative action afterwards; as one chief executive described:

> I have learnt a lot about getting over-stressed, what stresses me and how to avoid it. For example, I realize that having a backlog of work is the worst thing. I get really stressed if I have not read the paperwork for a meeting...I have got to keep up with all the issues, so if I take time off, which people advise me to do, then it actually makes things worse...I have also realized that I simply must have seven hours sleep at least five nights a week. And I have also cut down on drinking when I am stressed.

You also need to learn what relaxes you and try to ensure that you get the relaxation you need. Competitive sport may not be good relaxation when you are feeling stressed. There are various sources of help for stress: books, relaxation classes and tapes and individual counselling.

Use the ideal for understanding and managing yourself as a check list to see whether you need to improve. If so, use the next chapter as a guide to developing yourself.

UNDERSTANDING THE JOB AND BEING MORE EFFECTIVE IN IT

All except the best organized managers need to lift themselves occasionally out of their immersion in immediate tasks and problems to take stock of what they are doing. This section aims to help you to think about the nature of your job and the scope that you have to realize your vision. It provides different ideas and models for thinking about how you tackle your job. They have all been used by other managers and found helpful. However, individuals differ so that you are likely to find some of them more illuminating than others.

Managers vary in how they learn: some are analytical and can easily learn by reading and reflection; some are very practical and learn mainly by doing and finding out whether it works or not. Most managers are in between: they are primarily practical in their approach to their job but do welcome learning of new ways of understanding their situation so that they can control it better. This section is addressed to the latter group as well as to the analytical manager.

1. **Demands, constraints and choices**. Job descriptions can, at best, only give a very limited picture of a job. They do not capture the reality of a changing situation, the complexity of relations with individuals and groups, nor the scope that exists for jobholders to concentrate on particular aspects of the job. So *each jobholder has to discover what the job is like. This is a personal discovery,* as shown by the great variations in the kind of work that is done by people in similar jobs. It was finding out by observation just how great these variations are that helped the author to develop the demands, constraints and choices model to explain why and how this happened.[2]
    People do jobs differently because their abilities vary, but also because they see different things as being important, interesting or enjoyable. They notice different things, as anyone following managers in similar jobs who are doing a tour of the workplace will soon discover.

    These variations, in what people in similar jobs can do, mean that **managerial jobs offer considerable scope for individuals to choose what they do**. Two jobholders can focus their attention on different parts of the job. One, for example, may mainly concentrate on their staff and the work that they are doing, while another may spend most of the time on working with other people. The model of demands, constraints and choices provides a graphic way of thinking about how you can best use the opportunities that exist in your job to decide what work you think is most important. It is illustrated in Figure 13.1.

    The Figure 13.1 shows the *core of the job*, labelled 'demands', – that is, the work that anyone in the job would have to do, because they

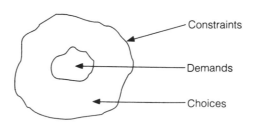

FIGURE 13.1   Model of a job: demands, constraints and choices

could not survive in the job unless it was done. These are the *tasks that you cannot neglect or delegate*. The figure also shows an outer boundary of *constraints* that limit what the jobholder can do, and an area of choices that are the work that one person in the job may do and another may not.

A major choice in all junior and middle management jobs – and even to a lesser extent in some senior ones – is how much time the manager spends in operational work, doing what he or she was originally trained to do. In the case studies, Heather-Jane in the first part talks about that and the reasons for getting so involved.

The lines in the diagram are uneven to indicate that all three parts of the diagram can change: a new boss may bring fresh demands, new constraints may appear, such as new legislation, or the manager may choose to try and reduce one of the constraints, such as attitudes opposing a change, and succeed in doing so. Changes in demands and in constraints can affect the amount and nature of the choices available. Different jobs will vary in how large or small is the core of demands, but in all there will be scope for choice. In senior management jobs there is a very large area of choice.

The choices that you exercise – though often you may not do so consciously – are what you focus your attention upon. One simple way of discovering this is how your time is divided between different categories of contacts. Figure 13.2 shows a way of thinking about how you divide your time between different kinds of contacts.

People not only do jobs differently they also see them differently. It can be liberating to recognize that how you see your job is very personal and may impose quite unnecessary limitations upon what you can do. One manager, for example, will think that much more of the job consists of inescapable demands while another will recognize how much choice the job offers in practice. Similarly, people in the same job may have a very different view of the constraints that limit what they can do. Some people feel hemmed in by constraints so that there is little they think they can do, whereas another person in the same job will see fewer constraints and seek to test troublesome constraints to see if they can be overcome. To quote John Harvey-Jones again:

> ...one of my personal invariable rules is that when I have mentally decided that something cannot be done, for what appears to be a very good reason, I test that apparent constraint, hopefully to destruction.[3]

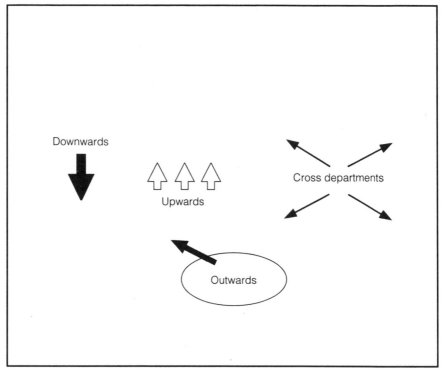

Downwards

Cross departments

Upwards

Outwards

FIGURE 13.2   Who gets most of your attention?

The framework of demands, constraints and choices can help you in thinking about personal priorities: whether some of the work that you do is indeed a demand, that is **work you must do**, or really something that you have chosen to do. Recognizing the latter can be particularly valuable when the volume of work presses heavily, because it can show you where you may be able to cut back. If you look back at your engagement book you can ask yourself how much of your work was really a demand and if so, who imposed it, was it yourself? If yourself, is this something that you think you should continue to do?

2. **Domain**. The area in Figure 13.1, which is bounded by the constraints line, shows the job's potential domain or territory. In practice, many jobholders occupy a smaller domain – that is their sphere of influence is smaller. One departmental manager, for example, does not seek to influence his director, or to play any part outside his own department, whereas another may be actively interested in helping to shape wider policies; one ward manager exercises considerable influence over the consultants who work there, whereas another accepts a subservient role. Managers with the narrower view – and hence smaller

domain – are focusing their attention downwards, on their staff, rather than sideways, upwards and outwards to all those whose actions and attitudes can affect their work and the resources available to them.

Most managerial jobs in the NHS offer jobholders some choice as to whom they seek to influence and in how wide an influence they try to have. **The idea of 'domain' is useful for stimulating you to think how wide an area you should be active in if you are to achieve your vision and therefore who you should seek to influence.**

3. **Boundaries**. Your domain has a boundary, which in many jobs is partially flexible. Once you have decided how large you want your domain to be, you need to be sensitive to what is happening at its periphery. Are there threats to the boundary? If so, what can you do to forestall them? Alternatively, are there parts of the boundary that you want to extend, where you feel that a wider influence is necessary to achieve your goals.

For many managers their boss is, at least at first, the most important person to influence, particularly if he or she is, in their opinion, unduly restrictive of their activities. Often this is a question of establishing themselves as being reliable. How to do this may vary with each boss, so it is important to discover what he or she is looking for. Bob Grindrod in Case Study 3 discusses how one can seek to be helpful to one's boss.

Managers at any level may feel the need to extend their domain so that they can influence those outside their establishment who can help or hinder what they are trying to accomplish. Many managers in the NHS will seek to influence the policies and actions of the social services. Others will want to enlist the help of people in the community, just as Heather-Jane in Case Study 5a did to get help with her aim of making the daily lives of the elderly patients more interesting.

Thinking in terms of the boundary of your domain has another use, that of identifying where there may be difficulties in relationships. Organization structures create separate departments and separate levels; in doing so, boundaries are created between one type of work and another. These clarify what kind of work is to be done and by whom. However, they can easily create a feeling of 'we' and 'they', and hence of difficulties in relationships.

The ease with which people come to see some as 'we' and others as 'they' can be shown experimentally. In one evening a group of strangers divided into groups will come to identify with members of their own group and see the others as outsiders. Any manager planning a reorganization should remember that where divisions are made, boundaries are created with dangers of misunderstanding, even distrust. Where there is such a danger, or where the 'we and they' attitude already exists, it is important to facilitate informal contacts. Such contacts usually encourage people to feel friendly.

So far we have concentrated on understanding the nature of the job to help you to review how you do it. Now we turn to more specific ways in which you can seek to be more effective in your job.

4. **Time management**. The simplest place to start is with *how you actually spend your time*. Many people, studies suggest, have a distorted view of what they do, over-estimating the time that they spend on some activities and under-estimating that on others. So *keep a running record of what you are doing for a week or more; if you have a secretary she can do much of it for you. Check this against what you believe you are doing and what you think you ought to be doing.* The next stage is to check on how much time you are giving to particular activities or people and whether you are satisfied with this. You may remember the quotation in Chapter 2 from Tom Peters on the need to show that you really think a subject is important by visibly spending a lot of time on it.

A record of how you spend your time tells you about how you are dividing your time between different problems, activities and people. It enables you to ask yourself how much of the work you do you judge to be important. Such a record can also show you what the pattern of your day is like: Is it very fragmented? Are there lots of interruptions? How often do you interrupt yourself turning away from a difficult paper? How much time do you spend in your office? How often do you visit? These are examples of some of the questions that you could usefully ask yourself about what you actually do. Many managers after keeping a record of how they spend their time decide that they ought to make some changes.

The next step is to decide whether you need help or whether you can discipline yourself to make the necessary changes. Help comes in three main forms: courses on the management of time – their long-running popularity shows how common a problem it has always been; books[4] and personal assistance. Many managers can make better use of their secretaries who often have more of a capacity to act as personal assistants than is recognized and some of whom have much more organizing ability than their bosses! Many leaders need administrative help, even if they themselves have come from an administrative background. The ex-service recruits to general management brought with them an understanding of the importance of such staff support.

5. **Keeping in touch**. It is common for senior managers over the years to bemoan the fact that they do not spend enough time visiting their staff: a characteristic that was noted more than 40 years ago by Sune Carlson in a pioneering study of nine Swedish managing directors.[5] He also noted that they did less visiting than they thought. It seems to be something that leaders say they believe is important but in practice give it too low a priority for them to spend much time on. Visiting is more important for a leader than for someone who is managing without also leading. Leaders have a greater need to be in touch with what their staff are thinking, and to be seen around 'spreading the messages' that they want to put across. Clare Dodgson in Case Study 1 discusses the importance of this.

There are many other ways of keeping informed about what is happening, but few are substitutes for the wide informal personal contact that can be achieved by visiting your staff, especially if they are numerous and in different locations.

You should always be striving to have a better understanding of what people are really thinking. Srivasta and Barrett put it well:

> Organizations need to experiment continually with new ways to facilitate the expression of members' concerns and ideas and create processes that are occasions for discovery.

They go on to suggest that:

> ...organizations need to create an 'antiorganization', a 'time-out' in which anyone is free to say anything, an arena where members are free to parody the formal organization and everyone agrees not to take offense:...a chance to ...create a parody of the offical culture where members can laugh at their own conventions from a safe distance.[6]

An opportunity that is sometimes taken in Christmas parties.

It is all too easy to think in a stereotyped way about listening to what your staff are really thinking and about how you get across your messages to them. The common description for both is 'good communications' but you need to think creatively, as Srivasta and Barrett suggest, about how you are really going to achieve that in practice.

Time management and keeping in touch have been highlighted as two important areas where it is easy for you to take action. Even more important is it for you to use the points under 'the ideal', at the beginning of this chapter, as a checklist for reviewing where you need to improve. Then you can go back to consider how effective a leader you are by reviewing yourself against 'the ideal' in Chapter 1, and in 'the ideal' for your relationships discussed in subsequent chapters.

Summary

To be an effective leader you need to understand and manage yourself. You need also to understand your job and to be able to appraise the way that you tackle it.

THE IDEAL

(a)   Understanding and Managing Yourself

● you develop appropriate self-confidence;
● you understand your strengths and weaknesses;
● you understand how you work, particularly what aspects of the job you may overlook or ignore;
● you know when you are too stressed and take action;
● you are aware of what you still need to learn.

(b)   Understanding the Job and Being Effective in it

● you know what you are trying to achieve;
● you understand the scope and nature of your job and the key relationships;
● you can prioritize your work successfully,
● you are self-disciplined and do not evade difficult decisions;
● you can take a broad view of problems but can, when necessary, understand the detail;
● you manage your time well;
● and, of course, you have the social skills needed for leading in your different relationships.

DIFFICULTIES IN ACHIEVING THE IDEAL

There may, of course, be real difficulties in your situation – it would not be a challenging job unless this was true – but, *many of the difficulties may come from yourself.* These can include: lack of self-disicipline and poor organization; an attraction to work that should be done by your juniors; an inability to look at problems objectively; insufficient drive and energy or ambition for the achievement of your vision, and too little or too much self-confidence.

STEPS TOWARDS THE IDEAL

(a)   *Understanding and Managing Yourself*

● you may need to develop, or to maintain, your self-confidence. It is less likely, but possible, that you will need to avoid over-confidence;
● the more challenging your job the more important it is that you understand and manage your stress symptoms;
● use the ideal as a checklist to decide where you need to develop yourself.

(b)   *Understanding your Job*

● you will benefit from taking stock of how you see your job and how you are doing it. *Realize that your view of your job is a highly personal one.* You see it differently from another jobholder. You are focusing your attention on particular aspects of the job, that is you are making choices – though you may only partly recognize this – in what you do and what you do not do. It helps to review the choices that you are making and ask yourself whether they are currently the right ones? You should also subject what you see as your main constraints to a stringent review, to check how real they are.
● Consider the *domain* – that is, the territory that you occupy – and whether you need to try and extend it if you are to realize your vision. Think of your domain as having a boundary: do you need to protect any of your boundaries? Do you need to establish closer relations with those on the edge of your boundary?

(c)   *Being More Effective in the Job*

● improve your time management unless you are already very good at it;
● keep in touch with your staff; strive to improve your understanding of what they really think; make time to visit;
● use the ideal as a checklist for asking yourself how close you are to the ideal. Then turn to Chapter 14 to consider how you are going to develop yourself.

Developing yourself

'A new model of leadership that expresses an ethic of self-development is needed, not just at the top, but at all levels.'

(Michael Maccoby)[1]

'Perception is the first step towards knowledge.'

(John Locke)

Nowadays leaders need to develop themselves, both as leaders and as managers, if they are to cope successfully with the changes affecting them. The aim of this chapter is to help you to think what this means, and how you can best develop yourself – it is not about professional updating.

We are all partially blind: blind to ourselves, to others and to what is happening around us. **Part of developing yourself is improving your perceptions. It is recognizing what you did not see before. This is the most important – and the hardest – aspect of self-development. It is one where there is always more to learn**.

The district general managers, who were studied over two years, discussed what they realized that they had learnt during their first two years in the job. Often this was about recognizing *what they did not know*:

to discover in mid-life that there are all these things that you thought you knew and actually don't...is quite a revelation.[2]

I have learned a lot about the health service in the context of the wider world...I have been surprised, I think, at the amount that I have learned. I had never thought I was a particularly naive person but I have seen a lot more complexity... than I had realized existed.

I, like most NHS chief officers and probably people in any discipline, made certain assumptions about my levels of understanding about the functions of other disciplines. I am now finding these assumptions were not terribly well founded so I need to spend time with my colleagues to make sure I understand enough of what their function is.

I have changed my approach to problems because I have learnt of the great gaps in my experience and I now seek out other perspectives more than I did.

The experience of leadership teaches you about yourself, as one of the tracer chief executives described:

What I have learned about myself and the enormous pressures and stress of the job has been an enormous amount.

The young leaders in Chapters 10 and 11 also discuss what they have learnt.

Experience can be a great teacher – but, like other forms of teaching, how much you learn depends *upon yourself.*

Self development means taking responsibility for your own learning, and helping others to develop themselves.[3] The idea of self development has been popular since the 1970s for the following reasons:

1. Recognition of the limitations of what can be accomplished by traditional training programmes.
2. More awareness of how people differ in personality, training and experience, and hence the need for more individualized development.
3. The trend towards greater participation and personal autonomy.
4. The economies of do-it-yourself training.
5. The development of training methods that make it easier for individuals to learn on their own via TV, videos and computers.
6. The need for individuals to assume more responsibility for managing their own careers, because of the decline in job security, and the greater mobility within and between organizations.

It is easy to think of learning too narrowly as just formal education, but it is much wider that that. It includes:

● updating knowledge;
● learning about new subjects and techniques that are relevant to your work;
● improving your skills, particularly your social skills;
● exploring good practice elsewhere;
● learning more about the environment within which you work;
● developing your understanding of the interests, attitudes and problems of the people who can affect your job;
● understanding yourself better, your strengths and weaknesses, and how your behaviour is seen by others; learning to manage yourself better.

The ideal

That you will:

1. recognize the need for continued learning;
2. accept responsibility for your own learning;
3. recognize how easy it is to get bogged down in your work, particularly in immediate problems, and take steps to try and counteract this;
4. understand what best stimulates you to learn, and seek out such stimulus while trying to remain open to other ways of learning;
5. think broadly about what 'learning' means;
6. learn from your failures as well as your successes.

You need to want to learn, and to *know how* to learn.

You should think broadly about what learning means so that you can make good use of all the varied opportunities that there are to do so. Some people show a greater capacity for learning from what happens to them than do others. The ideal is that you should be able to learn from your experiences.

Difficulties in achieving the ideal

Reading the ideal should immediately suggest some of the potential difficulties. There are four main ones:

1. Accepting that you *still need to learn*, and that you *can* still learn, even if you are experienced in your work and no longer young.
2. Thinking sufficiently broadly about learning: it is easy to accept that you need to learn a new technical skill for which you can see an immediate use, but harder to accept that broadening your understanding is a useful form of learning.
3. Accepting that learning is sufficiently important to make time both for formal learning and for activities that stimulate you to think afresh.
4. Not knowing how to learn: you may have too narrow a learning repertoire (this is explained below).

There may be other difficulties, too: you may have been too long in the same job to find it stimulating – though with all the reorganizations this is unlikely to be a problem; you may have a heavy but unchallenging workload; you may work for a boss who you think constrains you unduly; no-one may have tried to help you to develop; or you may have reacted against your experience of management education, and you may have difficult home circumstances that restrict your ability to develop yourself outside working hours.

There are also potential difficulties for your boss, even if he or she is interested in management development. One is making time to think about, and try to contribute to, your development. Another difficulty is accepting the value of self-development in practice. It is always a temptation to believe that one knows best what is good for other people.

There are fewer difficulties if you are young because you are more likely to accept that you need to learn, and others will be more aware that they should help you, and more motivated to do so.

Steps towards the ideal

The first step, at any age, is to *recognize the need to learn*

The most powerful motivation for learning is a need to know. This can be triggered by failure, which is why failure can be such a fruitful stimulus for learning unless it is explained away by rationalizations. If, for example, you did not get selected for a job that you wanted, ask yourself if the selectors may have been right not to choose you?

Another reason for needing to know is recognizing a gap between what you are and what you need to be to fill your current or desired job satisfactorily. If you are satisfied with your own performance, you will see little need to learn. If so, your first step towards the ideal is to develop higher standards for your performance, and to recognize what you do not know. You may also need a more realistic assessment of your performance.

FOR THE YOUNG

1. **Seek to understand the kind of person that you are**: what are your strengths and weaknesses, what is distinctive about the way that you interpret what is happening and in how you relate to other people? There are a variety of personality tests, such as the Myers-Briggs[4] that can help you, and a good many short programmes. Many companies run assessment centres that can be very helpful guides to your career potential, and so do some regions in the NHS. If you want a do-it-yourself analysis, a helpful book is Pedler, Burgoyne and Boydell, *A Manager's Guide to Self-Development.*[5]
2. **Consider what you can do to overcome, or at least to *lessen*, your weaknesses,** and consult whoever you find helpful about how to do this.

3. **Look for an older manager who can act as your guide** – now often called a mentor.

4. **There are many skills that a manager needs that can be improved by watching others** – for example, chairing; how to say 'no' without causing offence; how to organize your time; and how to make your expectations clear. So look out for people who are good at one or more of these skills, and study how they do it.

5. **Ask yourself who are the leaders**, or who show leadership abilities, in a particular situation? Why is it that others accept their leadership? **What can you learn from what they do?**

6. **Think about what you want from your career.** Review your qualifications and consider what others are necessary, or might be helpful, and plan how studying for these can be fitted in with your other commitments. Note how much part-time study a number of the managers in the case studies have done.

7. **Ask yourself what you are doing outside work that contributes to your development**, and whether you should consider doing more. Such rounded development is very much part of the 'university ideal', but the pressure of starting work, learning a new job and setting up a home can easily lead to a much narrower range of interests than at university – do-it-yourself around the house will not do much to develop you as a leader in the NHS, but active involvement in community work and team sports can give you opportunities to practise leadership skills. However, the long hours that many NHS managers are now working make this more difficult. There may – probably should – be times when domestic commitments preclude external activities as well as a job, so you need to make good use of the time before and, when you are older, after your family has grown up.

8. **Consider going on a leadership development course**: there are many different kinds including those that test you in hard physical conditions. Weigh up the usefulness of such courses and be prepared to pay for yourself if you cannot get funded by any other source.

9. **Recognize what stimulates you to learn, but try to broaden the ways that you learn.** Kolb's[6] widely quoted classification of learning methods can help you to analyse how you learn. Kolb argues that learning is a four stage process, but that people tend to be stronger at one or two stages and give inadequate attention to the others. The four stages are:

(a) Concrete experience (*doing*);
(b) Reflective observation (*reviewing*);
(c) Abstract concepts and generalization (*analysing*);
(d) Active experimentation (*trying it out*).

The four stage learning model provides a way of thinking about how to widen your learning repertoire by practising the stages that you *tend to ignore*. Some people, for example, are weak at reflective observation so if they make a mistake or are unsuccessful in achieving one of their aims they do not reflect on why that has happened. Others analyse but do not try out their conclusions. The use of the four stages of learning is illustrated below.

FOR THE MIDDLE WORK YEARS

1. Consider which of the suggestions for the young **should still apply to you**.
2. Now is a good time to **review your achievements against your expectations**, and to consider what you want from your future career. Developing yourself may be essential if you are planning a change of career, and will still be necessary if you expect to continue in the same way.
3. **This is often a good time to do something different, preferably a new job, but if not that, then look for other ways of challenging yourself to think and act differently.** Particularly if you are in a senior management post, you will benefit from finding somebody who can test your arguments and help you to think of new approaches. If there is no-one you feel that you can use in that way in your own organization, then look for someone outside. Additionally, establish an information exchange with your opposite number in another hospital/health authority/practice.
4. **Take part in some formal development activity each year**, whether it is a workshop, seminar, or course, but choose carefully. Aim to go to at least two, one to extend your knowledge of the health service and the other your knowledge of management. For the latter, widen your horizons by going, at least occasionally, to a programme that includes managers from outside the NHS.
5. **Visit other services like yours** elsewhere, and, if you can, health services in other countries. Use such visits as a way of consciously practising each part of the learning cycle:

(a) concrete experience – *impressions of the visit*;
(b) reflective observation – *reviewing what you noticed*;
(c) generalizations – what could or could not be *applied here*, and why?
(d) experimentation – *trying it out*.

FOR THE LATER WORK YEARS

Suggestions 3–5 above apply equally to you; suggestion 3 is especially important. Taking a very different type of job is remarkably revivifying, as the experience of many older managers shows. Failing that, **you need, even more than those in their middle years, to find people who will challenge your views** – the reason for the court jester – and to put yourself in new situations so that you are not too restricted to (and limited by) your customary ways of thinking and acting. One of the useful byproducts of all the reorganizations has been that most managers in the NHS have had to face the challenge of change.

FOR ALL

Reread the ideal and the common difficulties that may prevent you learning as much and as effectively as you could. **Recognize that learning is not just formally acquiring new knowledge and qualifications, or even seeking new job challenges, it is also very much trying to enlarge your perceptions.** Hence the quotation from John Locke at the head of this chapter. We are all in danger of tunnel vision, in the way we see problems, possibilities and people. You should seek to enlarge your perceptions of all three. Doing so will enhance your leadership abilities. It will do so even more if you can ally these four 'Ps' with three others: proactivity, planning and persistence, so as to progress your vision of the ideal. The sequence is shown in the 8Ps diagram in Figure 14.1.

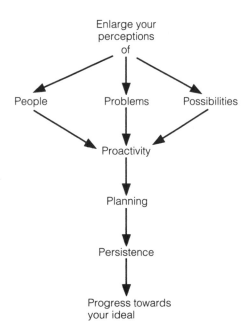

FIGURE 14.1   The 8Ps diagram

Summary

You should seek to develop yourself throughout your career so that you can lead and manage more effectively. *You should want to learn, and to improve your ability to learn.*

1. The most important part of developing yourself is *recognizing what you do not know.* There is always more to learn about:

- the context within which you work;
- the jobs of those you are trying to lead;
- understanding other people's attitudes;
- understanding yourself.

2. You should consciously try to learn, and to improve your ability to learn.
3. If you are young:

- seek to understand your strengths and weaknesses, and *take action* to reduce your weaknesses;
- look for role models both for how to lead and for specific skills;
- plan what you should learn to meet your career ambitions;
- seek out opportunities to practise leadership, both at work and in your leisure activities.

4. If you are no longer young:

- do something different, preferably a new job, that challenges you;
- take part every year in formal development activities;
- visit other health services; review what you learn and apply it.

5. For all: apply the 8Ps diagram.

In conclusion

The NHS needs leaders who can enthuse others with high goals for what they can achieve.

Do not have too grand an idea of leadership. You do not have to be charismatic but you must care – and care deeply – about what you want to achieve. You must show that you care in what you do, because you are a model for other people's actions.

Think boldly about what you and your group, large or small, should be trying to achieve. If you call it a vision, that will encourage you to be bold. Enlist others in building that vision.

Set high standards, and exemplify them. Be positive, for positive thinking spreads. Encourage others and when you feel discouraged keep it to yourself, or better share it with a trusted counsellor.

Leadership means enlisting others as willing cooperators. To do that you must recognize their importance and show that you consider them and their work important. You must also understand why their views may differ from yours and seek to find common goals. Above all, you must inspire trust: that is a key aspect of successful leadership in the NHS because there are so many individuals and groups who may be suspicious of you and your intentions.

A good leader should also be an effective manager. You will not be effective unless you are able to understand and manage yourself and your job.

You have to be willing to pay the price of leadership: hard work, pressures, becoming tougher, handling the conflict – particularly in yourself, if you are clinically trained, between professional and managerial objectives – discouragement and loneliness. However, the price brings rewards, as you saw in the Case Studies in Part III, above all the feeling that you have made a difference. I hope that you will want to pay the price – or, if you are already doing so, that you have found some ideas and suggestions in this book to help you to lead even better.

Appendix A

Details of the Templeton Tracer Study of DGMs

This study was financed by the NHS Training Authority from April 1985 to the end of September 1987. The study was initiated and directed by Rosemary Stewart. Professor Derek Williams was consultant to the project, Dr John Gabbay and Sue Dopson were the full-time research associates and Peter Smith, of Ashridge Management College and an Associate Fellow of Templeton College, was a part-time research associate. Val Martin was the secretary to the project.

The study had four aims:

1. To understand the job of the newly appointed district general managers.
2. To identify the strengths and weaknesses of different approaches to doing the job.
3. To shed light on some of the key issues for effective general management in the NHS, with the emphasis on key relationships rather than on management processes such as planning.
4. To draw lessons that would help in the selection, development, evaluation and performance of general managers.

The research was published by the NHSTA as the Templeton Series on DGMs. The views expressed were those of the authors, and not necessarily of NHSTA. Nine Issues Studies were published in 1987–88, and mailed monthly to chairmen and DGMs.

1. DGMs and Chairmen: A Productive Relationship?
2. The DGM and Quality Improvement
3. DGMs and the DHA: Working with Members
4. Fully in the Picture? How DGMs Keep Informed
5. Managing with Doctors; Working Together?
6. DGMs and Region: Different Perspectives
7. DGMs and the Relationship between Districts and Units
8. Role and Progress of DGMs: An Overview
9. Learning to be a DGM (which included a Postscript: A Guide to the Selection of District General Managers and a Job Description for District General Managers to supplement the district's).

METHODS

A sample of 20 DGMs were followed for two years from the early months of their appointment. The first five DGMs were chosed, to be as varied as possible in their jobs, from a management programme for DGMs at Templeton College. The aim then was to get the study started before the full-time research associates could be appointed. The other 15 of the 20 were a stratified random sample designed to give the full sample maximum coverage of professional background and type of district. There was at least one member of the sample in every region in England and one in Wales. Four were from teaching districts.

The sample was stratified to ensure a much broader spread of career background than would have been obtained by a random sample. The sample consisted of: 7 administrators, 5 from outside the NHS (including 3 from the armed services), 2 treasurers, 2 community physicians, 2 nurses and 2 hospital consultants.

The district populations were relatively evenly spread from just over 100 000 to well over 500 000. Revenue budgets ranged from under £20 million to over £100 million. The demographic characteristics of the districts were represented in almost the same proportions as in the OPCS cluster of 'demographic families' for the country as a whole.

Throughout the two years, the DGMs were asked about their views on their job, and about what they were doing. They were also asked to describe what they thought had gone well and what had gone badly, and why. Semi-structured questions were used, some of which were changed over time. There were special initial and final interviews and in between lengthy quarterly interviews. There were frequent, and often lengthy, telephone interviews at times to suit the DGM, which ranged from 8.00 am to 9.00 pm. The average was 25 interviews with each DGM, with more frequent contact in the early months.

There were also interviews with chairs and with some of the DGMs' principal contacts; the latter to ask questions about the subject of particular Issue Studies. A meeting of the DHA and of the district management board was observed in each district, and so were a few special meetings or seminars. Relevant documents were studied and previous agendas of the district management team compared with current agendas of the district management board.

The participating DGMs said that they had found the research process helpful, because it stimulated them to take stock of what they were doing. It could also be helpful in difficult times to have a sympathetic listener.

Appendix B

Questions asked of young leaders

1. Previous jobs? How long on present job?
2. What did you find most different about it?
3. What/who helped you to get where you are? Can you give examples?
4. What advice would you give someone aspiring to get a job like yours?
5. What do you see leadership as being?
6. Can you give some examples of leadership actions that you have seen?
7. Do you think of yourself as a leader?
8. How do you try to lead? influence? inspire others? (whichever of those words you feel comfortable with)
9. Can you give examples of where leadership is required in your job?
10. Do you think of yourself as a role model (example)? If so, does that influence how you act? If yes, can you illustrate?
11. Do you see any of your activities outside work as being leadership ones?
12. (*For women*) Do you think women lead any differently? If yes, how? [*not used in text.*]
13. What do you feel you have learned as a leader?
14. Still need to learn?
15. Price and rewards of leadership.
16. Impact of reorganization upon your work.

Notes and references

1   LEADERSHIP

1.   Quoted by John Van Maurik, *Discovering the Leader in You* (London: McGraw-Hill, 1994) p. 6.
2.   Rosemary Stewart, *The Reality of Management*, 2nd edn (London: Heinemann and Pan, 1985), and *The Reality of Organizations*, 3rd edn (Macmillan, 1993).
3.   Warren Bennis and Burt Nanus, *Leaders: Five Strategies for Taking Charge* (New York: Harper & Row, 1985) pp. 89–90.
4.   Ibid., p. viii.
5.   Gareth Morgan, *Riding the Waves of Change: Developing Managerial Competencies for a Turbulent World* (San Francisco: Jossey-Bass, 1988).
6.   Warren Bennis, *The Unconscious Conspiracy: Why Leaders Can't Lead* (New York: AMACON, 1976) p. 15.
7.   Douglas McGregor, *The Human Side of Enterprise* (New York: McGraw-Hill, 1960) p. 48. McGregor distinguished between Theory X, which he called the traditional view of motivation that people disliked work and therefore had to be coerced and controlled, and Theory Y, which was that people will work willingly, in the right conditions.
8.   John Van Maurik, *Discovering the Leader in You*, p. viii.
9.   J. de Kervasdoue, J. R. Kimberley and V. G. Rodwin, *The End of an Illusion: The Future of Health Policy in Western Industrialized Nations* (Berkeley: University of California, 1984).
10.   Tom Peters, *Thriving on Chaos: Handbook for a Management Revolution*, (London: Macmillan, 1987) p. 416.
11.   Ibid., p. 414.
12.   John Harvey-Jones, *Making it Happen: Reflections on Leadership* (London: Collins, 1988) pp. 112–13.
13.   *Templeton Series on District General Managers*, directed by Rosemary Stewart, Issue Study No. 9, 'Learning to be a DGM' (NHSTA 1987–8).
14.   J. R. Meindl, S. B. Ehrlich and J.M. Dukerich, 'The Romance of Leadership', *Administrative Science Quarterly* (March 1985) pp. 78–102.
15.   Tom Peters and Nancy Austin, *A Passion for Excellence: The Leadership Difference* (London: Collins, 1985).

INTRODUCTION TO PART II

1.   John P. Kotter, *The General Managers* (New York: Free Press, 1982).
2.   John L. J. Machin and Charles H. S. Tai, 'Senior Managers Audit Their Own Communications', *Journal of Enterprise Management*, 2 (1979) pp. 75–85.

3. R. Beckhard, *Managing Change in Organizations: Participants' Work-book* (Cambridge, Mass.: Addison-Wesley, 1985); Roger Plant, *Managing Change and Making it Stick* (London: Fontana/Collins, 1987); T. Turrill, 'Change and Innovation: A Challenge for the NHS', *IHSM Management Series*, 10 (London: IHSM, 1986).

2 LEADING STAFF

1. Warren Bennis and Burt Nanus, *Leaders: Five Strategies for Taking Charge* (New York: Harper & Row, 1985) p. 80.
2. Readers who are unfamiliar with the word 'role' may wonder why it is sometimes used in place of 'job'. 'Role' means 'to play the part of', and is useful to convey that occupying a particular job can mean playing a particular role, as an actor does.
3. John Harvey-Jones, *Making it Happen: Reflections on Leadership* (London: Collins, 1988) p. 65.
4. Ibid., pp. 7–8.
5. Ibid., pp. 67–8.

3 LEADERSHIP AND NURSES

1. Tom Peters, *Thriving on Chaos: Handbook for a Management Revolution* (London: Macmillan, 1987).
2. Nursing and Midwifery Staffs Negotiating Council: Staff Side, *Action Towards Equality* (Nursing and Midwifery Staffs Negotiating Council: Staff Wide, 1992) p. 13, based on figures from the Department of Health, 1991.
3. Ibid, p. 4.
4. Jane Robinson, Philip Strong and Ruth Elkan, *Griffiths and the Nurses: a National Survey of CNAs*, Nursing Policy Studies Centre (University of Warwick, 1989).
5. Christine Hancock, 'Claiming the Right to Nurse', *Nursing Standard* (19 October 1994) vol. 9, no. 4.
6. Ibid.
7. The growing importance of nurses in primary care was recognized in *New World, New Opportunities*, the report of a task group set up to examine the implications for primary care nursing of the move towards more care in the community. Department of Health, NHS Management Executive, (March 1993).
8. Elizabeth McElkerney, 'Doctors in Management', *British Journal of Nursing* (1994) vol. 3, no. l, pp. 43–5.
9. King's Fund College, *The Professional Nursing Contribution to Purchasing*, (The King's Fund, 1992).
10. NHS Executive, *Building a Stronger Team: the Nursing Contribution to Purchasing* (Dept. of Health, 1994).
11. Michael Traynor, 'Stormy Weather', *The Health Service Journal* (June 30, 1944) vol. 104, no. 5409, pp. 22–3.
12. Joan Higgins, 'Reformed Characters', *The Health Service Journal*, (February 17, 1994) vol. 104, no. 5390, p. 33.
13. Department of Health, NHS Management Executive, *A Vision for the Future: The Nursing, Midwifery and Health Visiting Contribution to Health and Health Care* (Dept. of Health, 1993) p. v.

14.   David Benton, 'An Agent for Change', *Nursing Standard* (1993) vol. 8, no. 9, p. 20.
15.   NHS Executive, *Building a Stronger Team; the Nursing Contribution to Purchasing*, p. 23.
16.   Rosemary Stewart, Peter Smith, Jenny Blake and Pauline Wingate, 'The District Administrator in the National Health Service' (King Edward's Hospital Fund for London, 1980).
17.   Christine Hancock, 'Educate, Agitate, Organise', *The Health Service Journal* (November 4, 1993) p. 21.
18.   Ann Selby, 'More Practice', *The Health Service Journal* (March 19, 1992) p. 31.
19.   See note 15.
20.   Ian Seccombe, et al., *The Price of Commitment: Nurses' Pay, Careers and Prospects* (Brighton: Institute of Manpower Studies, 1993).
21.   Ian Seccombe and James Buchan, 'High Anxiety', *The Health Service Journal* (October 14, 1993) vol. 103, no. 5374, pp. 22–4.
22.   *A Vision for the Future*, see note 13.
23.   Anthony Palmer, Sarah Burns and Chris Bulman, *Reflective Practice in Nursing – The Growth of the Professional Practitioner* (1994, Blackwell Scientific).
24.   P. J. Hibbs, *Pressure Area Care for the City and Hackney Health Authority* (City and Hackney Health Authority, 1988) p. 3.
25.   Peter West and Jill Priestley, 'Money under the Mattress', *The Health Service Journal* (April 14, 1994) pp. 20–22.
26.   C. McLoughlin, 'Managing Change', paper for a RGM/DGM meeting, 3 December 1987.
27.   R.W. Revans, *Action Learning in Hospitals: Diagnosis and Therapy* (London: McGraw-Hill, 1974). Part 1 of the book was published in 1964 as *Standards of Morale*.

4   LEADERSHIP AND DOCTORS

1.   Ian Morrison and Richard Smith, 'The Future of Medicine', *British Medical Journal*, 309 (October 29, 1994) pp. 1099–1100.
2.   NHSTA, 'Doctors and Management Development: Policy Proposals from the National Health Service Training Authority' (NHSTA, 1988) p. 7.
3.   Allan Bruce and Sandra Hill, 'Relationships between Doctors and Managers: The Scottish Experience', *Journal of Management in Medicine* (1994) vol. 8, no. 5, p. 56.
4.   Ibid, p. 54.
5.   Sue Dopson, 'Management: The One Disease Consultants Did Not Think Existed', *Journal of Management in Medicine* (1994) vol. 8, no. 5, pp. 34–5.
6.   Advertisement in *The Health Service Journal* (April 14, 1994) p. 56.
7.   David Hunter, 'Paradigm Shift Lost?', *The Health Service Journal* (February 20, 1992) vol. 102, no. 5290.
8.   John Harvey-Jones, *Making it Happen: Reflections on Leadership* (London: Collins, 1988) p. 126.

5   SHARING THE LEADERSHIP: CHAIR AND CHIEF EXECUTIVE

1.   A more detailed analysis is given in Rosemary Stewart, 'Chairmen and Chief Executives: An Exploration of their Relationship', *Journal of Management Studies* (September, 1991) vol. 28, no. 3, pp. 511–28.

2.   *Templeton Series on DGMs*, directed by Rosemary Stewart, Issue Study No. 1, 'DGMs and Chairmen: A Productive Relationship?' (NHSTA, 1986).
3.   Ibid.

6   SHARING THE LEADERSHIP: TEAM WORKING

1.   Department of Health, *Review of the Wider Department of Health* (Leeds: Department of Health, 1994) p. iii.
2.   Derek French and Heather Saward, *Dictionary of Management*, 2nd edn (Farnborough, Hants: Gower, 1983).
3.   Rani Chaudhry-Lawton and Kevin Crane 'How Teamwork Pays Dividends', in *Managing 1994: The Competitive Edge*, ed. Robert Heller (London: Sterling Publications, 1994) p. 167.
4.   Andrew Sims and David Sims, 'Top Teams', *The Health Service Journal* (24 June, 1993) p. 30.
5.   R. Meredith Belbin, *Management Teams: Why They Succeed or Fail* (London: Heinemann, 1981). This was his original book which sparked the interest in identifying team roles. His most recent, which includes some changes to the roles, is *Team Roles at Work* (Oxford: Butterworth-Heinemann, 1993).
6.   Ibid.

7   LEADERSHIP AND THE BOARD

1.   Department of Health, *Working for Patients* (Her Majesty's Stationery Office, January 1989).
2.   Lynn Ashburner and Liz Cairncross, *Authorities in the NHS – Research for Action, Briefing 3, Health Authorities in Formation 1990/1* (Bristol, NHSTD, no date).
3.   Ewan Ferlie, Lynn Ashburner and Louise Fitzgerald, 'The Non Executive Director and the Board: Some Evidence from the NHS', in Paul Anand, Sue Dopson and J. McGuire, eds, *Implementing Health Reforms* (Basingstoke: Macmillan, in press).
4.   Ibid.
5.   Ibid.
6.   *Templeton Series on DGMs*, directed by Rosemary Stewart, Issue Study No. 3, 'DGMs and the DHA: Working with Members' (NHSTA, 1986) p. 7.
7.   Quoted in National Association of Health Authorities, 'Acting with Authority' (NAHA, 1986) p. 3.
8.   *Templeton Series on DGMs*, directed by Rosemary Stewart, Issue Study No. 3, pp. 6–7.
9.   Ferlie, Ashburner and Fitzgerald, see note 3, pp. xx
10.   Charlotte Williamson, 'Authority Members and Standards of Non-Clinical Care', *Hospital and Health Services Review* (January 1986) p. 19.
11.   Lynn Ashburner and Ewan Ferlie, 'Fast Forward', *The Health Service Journal* (6 Jan 1994) vol. 104, no. 5384, pp. 20–21.
12.   Charlotte Williamson, 'You are in my power', *The Health Service Journal* (17 March 1994) vol. 104, no. 5394, pp. 24–26.

8   LEADING IN THE REGIONAL OFFICE

1.   Department of Health, *Managing the New NHS* (Leeds: Department of Health, 1993), p. 6.

2.   From the passing of the legislation to abolish RHAs.
3.   Department of Health, *Managing the New NHS*, p. 9.
4.   Department of Health, NHS Executive, *Managing the New NHS: Functions and Responsibilities in the New NHS* (Leeds: Department of Health, July 1994), p. 10.
5.   Ibid., p. 11.
6.   Ibid., p. 13.
7.   Ibid., p. 23.
8.   Ibid., p. 26.

9   EXTERNAL LEADERSHIP

1.   John Harvey-Jones, *Making it Happen: Reflections on Leadership* (London: Collins, 1988) p. 224.
2.   A. F. Long and S. Harrison (eds), *Health Services Performance: Effectiveness and Efficiency* (London: Croom Helm, 1985) p. 102. Jack Hallas, *CHCs in Action: A Review* (London: Nuffield Provincial Hospitals Trust, 1976).
3.   Gordon Chase and Elizabeth C. Reveal, *How to Manage in the Public Sector* (Reading, Massachusetts, Addison-Wesley, 1983), p. 129.
4.   David King, 'Health', in Drew Clode, Christopher Parker and Stuart Ethrington, *Towards the Sensitive Bureaucracy: Consumers' Welfare and the New Pluralism* (Aldershot: Gower, 1987), p. 57.
5.   Chase and Reveal, see note 3, pp. 128–30.
6.   Long and Harrison (eds), see note 2, p. 102.
7.   King, see note 4, p. 64.
8.   Karin Eriksen, *Human Services Today*, 2nd edn (Reston, Virginia: Reston Publishing 1981).

13   MANAGING THE JOB AND YOURSELF

1.   Warren Bennis and Burt Nanus, see note 1, Chapter 2, p. 56.
2.   For a fuller account of how to use the demands and constraints model to look at how you do your job see, Rosemary Stewart, *Managing Today and Tomorrow* (Basingstoke, Hants: Macmillan, 1989; paperback edn 1991), Chapter 1. The original account of the model was in Rosemary Stewart, *Choices for the Manager: A Guide to Managerial Work and Behaviour* (Maidenhead, Berks: McGraw-Hill (UK), 1982).
3.   John Harvey-Jones, *Making it Happen: Reflections on Leadership* (London: Collins, 1988) p. 20.
4.   Useful how-to-do-it books on the management of time are published frequently and have basically similar messages, so see what is available in the bookshop or library. A different kind of book is Rosemary Stewart, *Managers and Their Jobs: A Study of the Similarities and Differences in the Ways Managers Spend Their Time*, 2nd edn (London: Macmillan, 1988), which reports a study of how 160 managers spent their time, illustrates different forms of diary-keeping and the lessons that the participant managers drew about using their time more effectively.
5.   Sune Carlson, *Executive Behaviour: A Study of the Workload and Working Methods of Managing Directors* (Stockholm: Strombergs, 1951).
6.   Suresh Srivasta and Frank J. Barrett, 'Foundations for Executive Integrity: Dialogue, Diversity, Development', in Suresh Srivastva and Associates,

Executive Integrity: The Search for High Human Values in Organizational Life (San Francisco: Jossey-Bass, 1988) pp. 298–9.

14 DEVELOPING YOURSELF

1. Michael Maccoby, *The Leader: A New Face for American Management* (New York: Simon & Schuster, 1981) p. 54.
2. This, and some of the following quotations are taken from Issue Study No. 9 'Learning to be a DGM', *Templeton Series on DGMs*, directed by Rosemary Stewart (NHSTA, 1987).
3. A useful collection of papers on self-development, given at a conference sponsored by the MSC in 1986, is Mike Pedler, John Burgoyne and Tom Boydell, *Applying Self-development in Organizations* (New York: Prentice-Hall, 1988).
4. Katherine C. Briggs, and Isabel Briggs Myers, *Myers-Briggs Type Indicator* (Palo Alto, California: Consulting Psychologists Press, 1976).
5. Mike Pedler, John Burgoyne and Tom Boydell, *A Manager's Guide to Self-Development*, 2nd edn (Maidenhead: McGraw-Hill, 1978).
6. D. A. Kolb, K. M. Rubin, and J. M. McIntyre, *Organizational Psychology: An Experimental Approach* (Englewood Cliffs, N.J.: Prentice-Hall, 1971).

Index